The Language of Jokes

In this highly readable and thought-provoking book, Delia Chiaro explores the pragmatics of word play, using frameworks normally adopted in descriptive linguistics. Using examples from personally recorded conversations, she examines in detail the narrative structures of various joke forms, while jokes are also analysed from a contrastive viewpoint. Chiaro explores degrees of conformity to and deviation from established conventions; the 'tellability' of jokes and the interpretative role of the listener; the creative uses of puns, word play and ambiguity; and the contrast between serious and humorous discourse. The emphasis in her analysis is on the sociocultural contexts for the production and reception of jokes, and she examines the extent to which jokes are both universal in their appeal, and specific to a particular culture.

The book argues convincingly that jokes have been neglected as rich sources of patterned creativity in language use, and will be of interest to students of both language and literature.

Delia Chiaro has extensive teaching experience in universities and institutes of further education. She has published numerous books and articles for both students and teachers of English as a foreign language and her particular interests lie in the analysis of non-literary texts.

The INTERFACE Series

A linguist deaf to the poetic function of language and a literary scholar indifferent to linguistic problems and unconversant with linguistic methods, are equally flagrant anachronisms. – Roman Jakobson
This statement, made over twenty-five years ago, is no less relevant today, and 'flagrant anachronisms' still abound. The aim of the INTERFACE series is to examine topics at the 'interface' of language studies and literary criticism and in so doing to build bridges between these traditionally divided disciplines.

Already published in the series:

NARRATIVE
   A Critical Linguistic Introduction
   Michael J. Toolan
LANGUAGE, LITERATURE AND CRITICAL PRACTICE
   Ways of Analysing Text
   David Birch
LITERATURE, LANGUAGE AND CHANGE
   Ruth Waterhouse and John Stephens
LITERARY STUDIES IN ACTION
   Alan Durant and Nigel Fabb
LANGUAGE IN POPULAR FICTION
   Walter Nash
LANGUAGE, TEXT AND CONTEXT
   Essays in Stylistics
   Edited by Michael J. Toolan

The Series Editor
Ronald Carter is Professor of Modern English Language at the University of Nottingham and was National Coordinator of the 'Language in the National Curriculum' Project (LINC) from 1989 to 1992.

The Language of Jokes

Analysing verbal play

Delia Chiaro

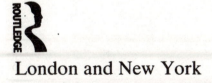

London and New York

First published in 1992 by Routledge
11 New Fetter Lane, London EC4P 4EE

Simultaneously published in the USA and Canada by Routledge
a division of Routledge, Chapman and Hall, Inc.
29 West 35th Street, New York, NY 10001

© 1992 Delia Chiaro

Set in 10/12pt Times by Florencetype Ltd, Kewstoke, Avon
Printed and bound in Great Britain by Clay Ltd, St Ives

British Library Cataloguing in Publication Data
Chiaro, Delia
    The language of jokes: analysing verbal play. – (Interface)
    I. Title   II. Series
    827.009

Library of Congress Cataloging in Publication Data
Chiaro, Delia
    The language of jokes: analysing verbal play/Delia Chiaro.
        p. cm. – (Interface)
    Includes bibliographical references and index.
    1. Joking. 2. Play on words. 3. Pragmatics. I. Title. II. Series: Interface
    (London, England)
    P304.C48 1992
    306.4'4–dc20   91–33616

    ISBN 0–415–03089–7
        0–415–03090–0 (pbk.)

Contents

Series editor's introduction to the Interface series

There have been many books published this century which have been devoted to the interface of language and literary studies. This is the first series of books devoted to this area commissioned by a major international publisher; it is the first time a group of writers have addressed themselves to issues at the interface of language and literature; and it is the first time an international professional association has worked closely with a publisher to establish such a venture. It is the purpose of this general introduction to the series to outline some of the main guiding principles underlying the books in the series.

The first principle adopted is one of not foreclosing on the many possibilities for the integration of language and literature studies. There are many ways in which the study of language and literature can be combined and many different theoretical, practical and curricular objects to be realized. Obviously, a close relationship with the aims and methods of descriptive linguistics will play a prominent part, so readers will encounter some detailed analysis of language in places. In keeping with a goal of much work in this field, writers will try to make their analysis sufficiently replicable for other analysts to see how they have arrived at the interpretative decisions they have reached and to allow others to reproduce their methods on the same or on other texts. But linguistic science does not have a monopoly in methodology and description any more than linguists can have sole possession of insights into language and its workings. Some contributors to the series adopt quite rigorous linguistic procedures; others proceed less rigorously but no less revealingly. All are, however, united by a belief that detailed scrutiny of the role of language in literary texts can be mutually enriching to language and literary studies.

Series of books are usually written to an overall formula or design. In the case of the Interface series this was considered to be not entirely appropriate. This is for the reasons given above, but also because, as the first series of its kind, it would be wrong to suggest that there are formulaic modes by which integration can be achieved. The fact that all the books address themselves to the integration of language and literature in any case imparts a natural and organic unity to the series. Thus, some of the books in this series will provide descriptive overviews, others will offer detailed case studies of a particular topic, others will involve single author studies, and some will be more pedagogically oriented.

This range of design and procedure means that a wide variety of audiences is envisaged for the series as a whole, though, of course, individual books are necessarily quite specifically targeted. The general level of exposition presumes quite advanced students of language and literature. Approximately, this level covers students of English language and literature (though not exclusively English) at senior high-school/upper sixth-form level to university students in their first or second year of study. Many of the books in the series are designed to be used by students. Some may serve as course books – these will normally contain exercises and suggestions for further work as well as glossaries and graded bibliographies which point the student towards further reading. Some books are also designed to be used by teachers for their own reading and updating, and to supplement courses; in some cases, specific questions of pedagogic theory, teaching procedure and methodology at the interface of language and literature are addressed.

From a pedagogic point of view it is the case in many parts of the world that students focus on literary texts, especially in the mother tongue, before undertaking any formal study of the language. With this fact in mind, contributors to the series have attempted to gloss all new technical terms and to assume on the part of their readers little or no previous knowledge of linguistics or formal language studies. They see no merit in not being detailed and explicit about what they describe in the linguistic properties of texts; but they recognize that formal language study can seem forbidding if it is not properly introduced.

A further characteristic of the series is that the authors engage in a direct relationship with their readers. The overall style of writing is informal and there is above all an attempt to lighten the usual style of academic discourse. In some cases this extends to the way in which notes and guidance for further work are presented. In all cases, the style adopted by authors is judged to be that most appropriate to the mediation of their chosen subject matter.

We now come to two major points of principle which underlie the conceptual scheme for the series. One is that the term 'literature' cannot be defined in isolation from an expression of ideology. In fact, no academic study, and certainly no description of the language of texts, can be neutral and objective, for the sociocultural positioning of the analyst will mean that the description is unavoidably political. Contributors to the series recognize and, in so far as this accords with the aims of each book, attempt to explore the role of ideology at the interface of language and literature. Second, most writers also prefer the term 'literatures' to a singular notion of literature. Some replace 'literature' altogether with the neutral term 'text'. It is for this reason that readers will not find exclusive discussions of the literary language of canonical literary texts; instead the linguistic heterogeneity of literature and the permeation of many discourses with what is conventionally thought of as poetic or literary language will be a focus. This means that in places as much space can be devoted to examples of word play in jokes, newspaper editorials, advertisements, historical writing, or a popular thriller as to a sonnet by Shakespeare or a passage from Jane Austen. It is also important to stress how the term 'literature' itself is historically variable and how different social and cultural assumptions can condition what is regarded as literature. In this respect the role of linguistic and literary theory is vital. It is an aim of the series to be constantly alert to new developments in the description and theory of texts.

Finally, as series editor, I have to underline the partnership and co-operation of the whole enterprise of the Interface series and acknowledge the advice and assistance received at many stages from the PALA Committee and from Routledge. In turn, we are all fortunate to have the benefit of three associate editors with considerable collective depth of experience in this field in different parts of the world: Professor Roger Fowler, Professor Mary Louise Pratt, Professor Michael Halliday. In spite of their own individual orientations, I am sure that all concerned with the series would want to endorse the statement by Roman Jakobson made over twenty-five years ago but which is no less relevant today:

> A linguist deaf to the poetic function of language and a literary scholar indifferent to linguistic problems and unconversant with linguistic methods, are equally flagrant anachronisms.

The Language of Jokes may not appear an obvious candidate for inclusion in a series of books concerned with the interface between language and literary studies. Jokes are certainly not part of a canonical tradition of literature with a capital L, nor are they normally considered to be contexts of language use which may have 'literary' applications.

In this book Delia Chiaro reveals much that is of interest to students of both language and literature and convinces us that jokes have been neglected as rich sources of patterned creativity in language use. Dr Chiaro demonstrates her case through a detailed and systematic attention to language functions which have parallels in more traditional contexts of literary study. The diverse range of material treated includes: the narrative organization of jokes; degrees of conformity to and deviation from established conventions; the 'tellability' of jokes and the role of the reader/listener in interpreting them; discourse strategies in making jokes; the creative uses of puns, word play and ambiguities. The emphasis in Dr Chiaro's argument falls increasingly on sociocultural contexts for the production and reception of jokes, and she explores the extent to which jokes are both universal in their appeal and specific cultural artefacts, embedded within and representing different cultural assumptions.

To this highly readable study, Delia Chiaro brings a seriousness of mind and playfulness of style which befits a subject which is now likely to be studied further as a result of her work.

Ronald Carter

Introduction

Studies on humour and what makes people laugh are countless. Over the centuries, writers of diverse interests have attempted to define it, supply reasons for it, analyse it. From Plato and Aristotle to Cicero, through Hume and Kant to the more recent Bergson and Freud, the resulting bibliography provides us with as many theories as there are theorists. Nevertheless, most works on humour tend to be concerned with themes such as its physiological, psychological and sociological aspects and few scholars in comparison have worked on the linguistic aspects of the comic mode.

Naturally, most major works on language do include something on verbal humour, but the norm tends to be the inclusion of a page or two which play mere lipservice to phenomena such as metathesis, polysemy, homophony and so on. On the other hand, linguists such as Charles Hockett, Harvey Sacks and Joel Sherzer have taken a deeper interest in word play, producing what must be the only truly seminal works on the language of jokes, while it has only been of late that entire books dedicated to the language of humour have appeared (e.g. Walter Nash, Walter Redfern). Perhaps the lack of abundance of major works in the field could be due to the fact that there is a widespread feeling that academic respectability is directly correlated to unenjoyable subject matter, thus the study of humour, by its very nature, cannot be taken seriously. On the other hand, in an era in which scholarly books on phenomena connected to mass media such as soap opera, quiz shows and football matches have given rise to the discipline of media studies, it may be the case that we are ready to accept books on verbal humour which do not need to be justified by psychological or philosophical whys and wherefores and examples taken from traditional literature.

From John o'Groats to Land's End word play appears to be one of the nation's favourite pastimes. The term word play includes every conceivable way in which language is used with the intent to amuse. Word play stretches way beyond the joke which, in itself, is indeed a handy container in which such play may occur, but this blanket term also covers the sort of *double entendre* which is so common in conversation, public speeches, headlines and graffiti, not to mention the works of famous punsters such as Shakespeare and Joyce.

British humour attracts and mystifies non-natives of the British Isles. The notoriety of the British sense of humour is as widespread as tea at five o'clock and stiff upper lips, although possibly not as mythical. A glance at the shelves of any bookshop will reveal a marked preference for the comic genre: written spin-offs of situation comedies, books by well-known comedians, collections of jokes and compendiums of rhymes and riddles for children. Such literature undoubtedly interests a large sector of the nation's reading public while more 'serious' humour can be found amongst the classics. If Britain's more high-flown literature envies others their Balzacs and Dostoevskys, as far as the comic mode is concerned, it remains quite unrivalled. There are, in fact, hardly any writers in English literature who have not attempted at least once to be funny with or through the medium of words.

This book will not be dealing with the eminent punsters of the literary world, but with the nation's unknown jokers. The anonymous authors of countless millions of quips, asides, graffiti and rhymes are rarely considered worthy of serious study; in fact, people would probably consider such instances of language as insignificant. However, the sprawling mass which is word, or verbal, play can be ordered and classified in such a way as to show that the linguistic options available to the joker are no different from those available to the poet. Of course, taxonomies of word play already exist (e.g. Hockett, 1977; Alexander, 1981; Nash, 1985) as do analyses of the narrative structure of jokes. On the other hand, we know very little of the interactive processes involved in word play. Although we know that it is particularly pervasive in British culture, we hardly know why it nonplusses foreigners both at a formal level and at an interactive level. Furthermore, few studies have been carried out which consider word play in contrast across languages.

We shall thus try to go one small step further than the existing literature on word play by considering what occurs outside the humorous text, how people react and interact in the face of verbal play and where, if anywhere, lies the cut-off point between serious and humorous discourse.

The examples in the book have either been taken from collections of jokes or else retrieved from my memory; others still have been recorded at dinner parties while speakers were unaware that they were being recorded. However, most frequently, especially with regard to the chapter on interaction, I have had to work from memory. Predicting when someone is going to be funny is not always possible and this has, of course, caused a few inevitable inaccuracies; these should not, however, detract from the gist of the analyses.

Acknowledgements

I would first like to thank all the colleagues, students and friends who have unwittingly or otherwise contributed to this book; in particular, researchers of the Cobuild Dictionary working at Birmingham University in the summer of 1985 and those present at the numerous informal gatherings during the AIA conference in Turin later that same year, especially Wanda d'Addic and John McRae. I am also grateful to Charmaine Lee, Denise Poole and the French, Spanish, German and Russian *lettori* of the Istituto Universitario Orientale, Naples, who helped me 'get' jokes in their respective languages. I would also like to thank Sarah Pearsall for her endless patience with me and the British/Italian postal services.

Last but not least, my thanks go to Malcolm Coulthard who, so long ago, helped me clarify my somewhat confused thoughts on puns and word play as well as encouraging me to continue in my research; and to Ron Carter for his invaluable comments and criticisms during the various stages of the preparation of the manuscript.

1   About word play

The term word play conjures up an array of conceits ranging from puns and spoonerisms to wisecracks and funny stories. Word play is, in fact, inseparably linked to humour which in turn is linked to laughter; so in a book which sets out to explore such a subject, it is hard to resist not to begin by pointing out the obvious analogy which exists between language and laughter, the fact that both are human universals.

> In all its many-splendoured varieties, humour can be simply de-fined as a type of stimulation that tends to elicit the laughter reflex. Spontaneous laughter is a motor reflex produced by the coordi-nated contraction of 15 facial muscles in a stereotyped pattern and accompanied by altered breathing. Electrical stimulation of the main lifting muscle of the upper lip, the zygomatic major, with currents of varying intensity produces facial expressions ranging from the faint smile through the broad grin to the contortions typical of explosive laughter.
>
> (Koestler, 1974)

The physiological processes involved in the production of laughter described above are identical in men and women the world over. Equally complex physiological processes underlie the formation of speech sounds. In fact, from Birmingham to Bombay the formation of speech sounds is simply variations of identical physical procedures involving the various speech organs; in other words, as far as laughing and speaking are concerned, we all do it in the same way. However, the comparison between laughter and language cannot be developed any further, for, if it were, then, just as different languages are simply manifestations triggered off by the universal blueprint of a single grammatical matrix, it should follow that all laughter has a single stimulus. Where laughter is concerned, however, the process is reversed; while the physical manifestation of laughter is the same the world over, its stimulus differs from culture to culture.

It is a well-known fact that the same things are not funny to everybody. We have all at some time made what we consider to be a witty remark at the wrong time and in the wrong company and have consequently had to suffer acute embarrassment to find the joke falls flat. Tacit rules underlie where, when and with whom it is permissible to joke. What is more, what may appear to be funny at a certain moment in time may cease to be so a few months later. If we then begin to consider the exportability of funniness, we will soon find that a traditional vehicle of humour such as the joke does not generally travel well. The concept of what people find funny appears to be surrounded by linguistic, geographical, diachronic, sociocultural and personal boundaries.

The notion of humour and what makes people laugh has intrigued scholars of various disciplines for centuries. Philosophers, psychologists and sociologists have attempted to define the whys and wherefores of humour and, above all, its essence. Such studies have resulted in numerous theories on the subject, some of which are more convincing than others; yet in their quest for a reason why, students of humour have tended to lose sight of the ways in which humorous effects are achieved. In fact, while considerable interest has been aroused by the subconscious processes concealed behind a burst of laughter or a smile, the stimulus itself has been largely ignored, rather as though unworthy of serious consideration.

Word play, the use of language with intent to amuse, is, of course, only one of numerous ways of provoking laughter. Although at first sight it may appear to be convenient to detach it from non-verbal stimuli, this soon proves to be an impossible task due to the fact that word play is inextricably linked to circumstances which belong to the world which exists beyond words. While it is perfectly possible to stimulate laughter without words, once words become part of the stimulus, whatever the type of verbal conceit, it is bound to be the verbalization of a state, an event or a situation. Over and above this, although the manipulation of the language itself may well be involved in the creation of a stimulus, instances of word play in which the language is used as an end in itself with the aim of amusing would be a contradiction in terms.

BEYOND WORDS

Everyone is capable of producing laughter, yet different people are amused by different things, so let us try to identify what, if anything, may be considered funny universally. There are situations which may be seen as funny in all western societies. Practical jokes such as pulling a chair away when someone is about to sit down are a pretty universal source of amusement to schoolchildren, while other stock examples include seeing someone slip on a banana skin or receive a custard pie in the face.

Henri Bergson, in his famous essay *Le Rire*, in an attempt at explaining why we laugh, concluded that we always laugh at 'something human', at 'inelasticity', at 'rigidity' and 'when something mechanical is encrusted on something that is living'. In this light we can perhaps explain the laughter triggered off by the clumsiness of a clown or the mishaps of a comic like Buster Keaton. Yet on the other hand, it may be equally feasible to suggest that laughter is triggered off by something which is not at all funny in itself, but which symbolizes a well-established comic pattern. After all, is there any real reason why Groucho Marx's cigar and raised eyebrows should make us laugh? Yet they do and they do so universally. Are we really simply laughing at his mechanistic movements? If we try to trace such a stimulus back to its source or primeval association in order to find an explanation we soon find ourselves involved in a complicated and possibly hopeless task.

Like Groucho Marx, Charlie Chaplin with his ill-fitting suit and rickety walk, the antics of Laurel and Hardy, and more recently the lecherous Benny Hill chasing lightly clad ladies around fields have all succeeded in amusing audiences despite geographical boundaries; yet where slapstick (and lewdness in the case of Benny Hill) stimulates laughter universally, other situations are only amusing well within the borders of their country of origin.

In Italy, for example, where most television situation comedies are imported from either Britain or the United States, a series is only successful if the situation depicted is not too culture-specific. For example, in the early 1980s the series *George and Mildred* and *Different Strokes* became extremely successful in Italy. Both programmes are basically farcical in structure with dramatic irony used as an indispensable feature in each episode. The main character is usually responsible for a misdeed which is worsened when he tries to remedy it. This results in situations which are not too different from the 'fine messes' in which Stan Laurel constantly involved Oliver Hardy. On the other hand, the problems of a priest trying to outdo his Anglican counterpart in a parish somewhere in England (*Bless me, Father*) are far too culture-specific to hope to amuse Roman Catholic Italy. In fact, the latter series was quickly relegated to off-peak viewing time on one of the country's minor commercial channels.

Situation comedy frequently plays on stereotypes. John Cleese's bowler-hatted business man (*Monty Python*) and hotelier (*Fawlty Towers*), members of the French resistance (*'Allo, 'Allo*) and typical British civil servants (*Yes, Prime Minister*) are all figures belonging to British culture which are instantly recognized in their inflated parodied forms by home audiences. Outside the British Isles, the stereotypes do not necessarily correspond as being comic in intent.

Situation comedies involve someone getting into some kind of mess. From the intricate farces of Plautus, through to the court jester and then the clown, from boss-eyed Ben Turpin to John Cleese's 'Silly Walks', from the ill-treated guests at Fawlty Towers to the painfully embarrassing situations created by *Candid Camera*, it would appear that people's misfortunes have always been a laughing matter. As far back as *Philebus* we find Plato claiming that:

> when we laugh at the ridiculous qualities of our friends, we mix pleasure with pain
>
> (1925: 338–9)

while Aristotle declares that:

> Comedy . . . is a representation of inferior people, not indeed in the full sense of the word bad, but the laughable is a species of the base or ugly. It consists in some blunder or ugliness that does not cause pain or disaster, an obvious example being the comic mask which is ugly and distorted but not painful.
>
> (1927: 18–21)

COMMON DENOMINATORS IN VERBAL HUMOUR

If we now turn to the field of verbal humour, we will find that the intrusion of language will restrict the stimulus to a smaller audience. Nevertheless, the topics of jokes tend to be universal. Degradation, for example, is the subject of an entire category of jokes. Physical handicaps which are the topic of 'sick' jokes may well appeal to feelings of repressed sadism, while most western societies possess a dimwitted underdog who is the butt of a whole subcategory of derogatory jokes which possibly allow their recipients to give vent to equally repressed feelings of superiority. The Irishman in England is transformed into a Belgian in France, a Portuguese in Brazil and a

Pole in the United States. All of them are victims of jokes in which they clearly become 'inferior people' in unlikely situations in which they display pure stupidity. The Polish captain in the following joke can be substituted by a captain of the 'inferior' group of one's choice in order to adapt it to a non-American audience:

J1
A Polish Airline passenger plane lands with difficulty on a modern runway just stopping short of disaster. The Polish captain wipes his brow after successfully braking the plane. 'Whew!' he says, 'that's the shortest runway I've ever seen.'
'Yes', says his copilot, looking wonderingly to his left and then to his right, 'but it sure is wide.'

Why it is that any minority ethnic group can find itself becoming the subject of a derogatory joke (and consequently laughed *at* by its recipients) may not, however, necessarily depend upon the inventor's hidden feelings of superiority. Over the years, practically every ethnic group in the United States has taken its turn at being the underdog. Recent literature on the subject (Bier, 1979 and 1988) suggests that it would be equally feasible to suggest that Blacks, Jews, Italians and Puerto Ricans may have presented both an economic and phallic threat to the white middle-class American, thus suggesting that such jokes conceal repressed feelings of fear and anxiety rather than superiority.

Minority groups do not however necessarily have to be of the ethnic variety in order to qualify as joke material. In Italy, the *carabinieri*, one of the country's three police forces, replace the ethnic stooge, while in Poland the role is played by the secret police. Other types of derogatory jokes involve cripples, the mentally sick, homosexuals, wives, mothers-in-law and women in general. Only recently, after the advent of feminism, have we begun to hear jokes in which men are the butt of derogatory humour:

J2
Q. *Why are women bad at parking?*
A. *Because they're used to men telling them that this much (joker indicates an inch with thumb and forefinger) is ten inches.*

This joke of course combines the put-down joke with another western joke universal: sex. Generally speaking, in 'civilized' societies dirty jokes are considered amusing especially if they concern newly-weds or sexual initiation. However, such jokes undergo variations from culture to culture. In many cultures, male prowess and penis size are a common feature of the 'dirty' joke, while in others, seduction, adultery and cuckolded husbands appear to amuse, and let us not forget that many people find other bodily functions funny too, so that 'lavatorial' jokes are far from being unusual, both among children and adults.

Many people would agree with Charles Lamb when he claims that: 'Anything awful makes me laugh' (letter to Southey, 9 August 1815); and Freud's idea of the child born free but who is forced into a state of repression within months of birth certainly rings true if we consider that by playground age a child is ready to giggle guiltily at a scurrilous remark. Later on in life we see that an important aspect of male camaraderie lies deeply ingrained in traditions in which the dirty joke reigns supreme – the rugby song and the banter and repartee of the working man's club and the stag night are just two examples. J2 upsets a rather male-centric tradition of dirty jokes by poking fun at the male. He is now forced to laugh at himself and his over-preoccupation with penis size and sexual performance. As for laughing at the underdog, who in this example is the male, surely here we laugh the self-satisfied laugh of he or she who knows better?

Alongside the topics of sex and underdogs, another common denominator which is universally present in jokes is what we shall term the 'absurd' or 'out of this world' element. Jokes containing such elements can be easily compared to fairy tales as both may be inhabited by humanized objects and talking animals. Throughout the duration of these jokes, the recipient's disbelief must be suspended in the same way as it is suspended in order to watch an animated cartoon in which famous cats like Tom and Sylvester get flattened by steamrollers, hit over the head by gigantic hammers and pushed off mountains, yet, nevertheless, always manage to survive and return for another episode.

J3
Jeremy Cauliflower is involved in a very bad car accident; sprigs are scattered all over the road and he is immediately rushed to hospital where a team of surgeons quickly carry out a major operation. Meanwhile, his parents, Mr and Mrs Cauliflower sit outside the operating theatre anxiously waiting for the outcome of the operation. After five hours one of the surgeons comes out of the theatre and approaches Jeremy's parents.

'Well,' asks Mr Cauliflower, 'will Jeremy live?'

'It's been a long and difficult operation', replies the surgeon, 'and Jeremy's going to survive. However I'm afraid there's something you ought to know.'

'What?' ask the Cauliflowers.

'I'm sorry,' replies the surgeon, 'we've done our best but . . . but I'm afraid your son's going to remain a vegetable for the rest of his life.'

The recipient of J3 does not question the fact that vegetables are referred to by name, are involved in car accidents and undergo major surgery. Being game to a world in which anything goes but which would be totally out of the question in reality by even the wildest stretches of the imagination, appears to be a tacit rule between joker and recipient.

THE CONCEPT OF SHARED KNOWLEDGE

We have already seen that when a comic situation is too culture-specific it will not be seen as amusing outside the culture of origin. It therefore follows that if a joke contains a situation which is heavily culturally oriented, it too will not travel well. Let us consider two translated jokes to demonstrate the importance of shared knowledge between sender and recipient in order for a joke to be understood. The first joke, J4, is translated from Italian:

J4
At a party in a luxurious villa, the host says to his playboy guest: 'See the women in this room? Except for my mother and my sister, I've been to bed with all of them.'

The irritated playboy retorts: 'Well then, that means that, between the pair of us, we've been to bed with them all!'

The joke is not a straightforward put-down as the playboy's answer might suggest to the non-Italian. At first the answer may appear to be a simple attempt at numerical one-upmanship but this interpretation ignores the underlying Italian sociocultural implications of sisters' and mothers' sexuality. In order to 'get' the joke completely, the recipient must be aware of the fact that, until quite recently, to some Italian men the purity of their mothers and sisters was unquestionable, and they could thus be cuckolded through their sexuality as well as through their wives' infidelity. Naturally, nowadays such a mentality is no longer widespread; in fact, it is highly unlikely to exist at all outside a few remote rural areas, yet it is still recognized as an Italian 'semi-myth' alongside those of the Latin lover and an exclusive diet of spaghetti. Whether it is funny or not, in Italy, the joke is certainly recognized as an attempt at being so. The following joke, which has been translated from Spanish, is equally restricted to a Spanish audience:

J5
During the Second World War, Hitler, Mussolini and Franco were travelling on the same plane. They were discussing the people they governed and

each of them claimed that his subjects were the most fervid patriots in the world. As the discussion got more and more heated they decided to resolve the question and see which people were, in fact, the most patriotic. The plane would fly over Berlin, Rome and Madrid, a feather would be dropped on each city and whoever it would fall on was to commit suicide, thus proving their total commitment to their country.

First, the plane flew over Berlin. A feather was dropped and after a few minutes a shot was heard.

'There you are!' said Hitler. 'The Germans are the most patriotic race in the world!'

Next, the plane flew over Rome. A feather was dropped and after a few minutes a shot was heard.

'There you are!' said Mussolini. 'The Italians are the most patriotic people in the world!'

Finally, the plane flew over Madrid. A feather was dropped. However, no shot was heard. The plane swooped down towards the city to see what had happened. Thousands of Spaniards were busy blowing the feather as far away from themselves as possible.

To the British recipient the joke is not amusing, as he or she is not likely to be aware of the Spanish habit of poking fun at themselves and at their poor sense of patriotism through the joke form. Furthermore, since British jokes in which the British are depicted as cowards are practically unheard of (it is in fact the Italians who are the cowards in British jokes), the text becomes quite meaningless through a lack of correspondence too.

If word play is to be successful, it has to play on knowledge which is shared between sender and recipient. Translated jokes like J3 and J4 require an explanation for a non-Italian or non-Spaniard to recognize them (in their entirety) as attempts to amuse, otherwise they will remain restricted to those who are *au fait* with all the underlying implications. British humour frequently intrigues non-native speakers of English and one of the reasons for their not appreciating it to the full is precisely due to a mismatch not only in language but also in shared sociocultural knowledge.

Therefore, the recipient of a joke must understand the code in which it is delivered and, although recognition of language is, of course, the lowest common denominator required for the comprehension of a joke, this recognition appears to include a large amount of sociocultural information which should also be in their possession. As we shall see from the examples that follow, such knowledge is extremely varied and ranges from mundane everyday experiences common to the culture of the language in which the joke is delivered to what we shall term as encyclopaedic or 'world' knowledge.

J4 and J5 clearly show how important it is to possess a knowledge of the 'world'. Linguistic competence in such jokes is the least of the recipient's problems. The same is true of J6.

J6
British Rail announced today that coffee was going up 20p a slice

(Barker, 1978)

To get J6, a great deal of knowledge regarding the quality of catering provided by British Rail is required; it is therefore restricted to those who have a sound knowledge and/or experience of refreshments served by British Rail. Of course, the joke could be explained by describing the temperature, colour, consistency and, above all, the freshness of the liquid in question. Although such an explanation would help the recipient towards an interpretation of the joke, a personal experience, even at hearsay level, may well prove essential to understanding exactly why British Rail coffee is likened to last week's loaf. What is more, the remark plays on implication, thus relying on pretty complex reasoning on the part of the recipient who wishes to work it out. (The chances are that, due to the lack of pragmatic signals, a not particularly proficient non-native speaker may not even recognize the remark as an attempt at being funny. This, of course, raises the question of how recipients, regardless of their mother tongue, recognize this fact. See Chapter 5.)

Sociocultural knowledge is, however, by no means restricted only geographically. A brief perusal of playground jokes collected by Opie and Opie in the 1950s clearly shows how joke material changes as time goes by. It is highly unlikely that schoolchildren of the 1990s will be familiar with Ian Christie, teddy boys or Davy Crockett (or with the theme song of the TV series, 'Davy, Davy Crockett, king of the wild frontier!') and therefore they probably will not get the puns on which the following examples play:

J7a
Q.   *If Christie had two sons what would he call them?*
A.   *Ropem and Chokem*[1]

J7b
Do you know a teddy boy's just been drowned – in his drainpipe trousers

(Opie and Opie, 1959: 106)

J7c
'How many ears has Davy Crockett?'
'Two, hasn't he?'
'No, three. He's got a left ear and a right ear and a wild frontier.'
(ibid.: 120)

The last example, J7c, shows that there is still a third factor to be considered. The recipient of a joke often needs to be able to recognize instances of broken (or merely bent) linguistic rules. In other words his/her linguistic knowledge requires a high standard of proficiency to be able to deal with the ambiguities and hidden traps of, in this case, the English language.

We can thus say that three systems interact with each other in order to make up the sort of competence required in order to get a joke: linguistic, sociocultural and 'poetic'. Richard Alexander (1982) defines poetic competence as the ability to recognize the ways in which linguistic options can be manoeuvred in order to create a desired effect – the recipient of a joke, in a sense, is in a similar position to the reader of poetry; both need to appreciate exactly how the comic/poet has toyed with the language.

J7c illustrates how the linguistic/sociocultural/poetic systems can act together to produce a joke which could only be understood by a rather proficient non-native speaker of English. However, the interaction of these systems may well create more complex problems for such a recipient:

J8
Sum ergo cogito
Is that putting Des-cartes before de-horse?

Sociocultural restrictions, as well as being geographical or historical, may also be of an intellectual variety. First, here we see that part of the attraction of this example is that it tests the reader's ability to spot the reference. It will only appeal to a limited audience who will have to unravel and actually work out a solution to the 'joke', rather as though they were solving a puzzle. In fact, in this case the reader has to (a) know the quotation, (b) see that it has been inverted, (c) know that Descartes was the author of the quotation and that he was French, (d) recognize the idiom in the punchline, and (e) link the marked form of 'the' /dɪ/ as indicative of a French accent. The recipient will need to possess an extremely proficient knowledge (which is usually totally subconscious in native speakers) of the inherent comic possibilities of the English language in order to perceive the allusive homophony involved: what we have defined as poetic competence.

Thus, if someone does not get a joke, this will be due to a certain amount of unshared knowledge between sender and recipient. Not getting a dirty joke may reveal gaps in sexual knowledge (it is not at all unusual for adolescents, for example, to laugh at sexual jokes even if they have not understood them, so as not to lose face with their peers); similarly, not seeing a literary reference may reveal a cultural lacuna (which may be equally well camouflaged before our intellectual peers if and when the need arises!); while not understanding why British Rail coffee is compared to stale bread simply demonstrates that the recipient has never travelled on trains in the United Kingdom. However, not getting a joke may also be due to linguistic limitations, as in the case of non-native speakers of English exposed to jokes like J8, which is doubly difficult to get because linguistic play intersects play on world knowledge. On the other hand, J8 is generally considered a good joke because it does indeed crosscut the language/world knowledge barrier. Cicero makes this very point in his distinction of these two types of humour:

> For there are two types of wit, one employed upon facts, the other upon words.
>
> *(De Oratore*, II, LIX, 239–40) (1965: 377)

> a witty saying has its point sometimes in facts, sometimes in words, though people are most particularly amused whenever laughter is excited by the union of the two.
>
> (II, LXI, 248) (1965: 383)

PROSAIC AND POETIC JOKES?

In his seminal paper on jokes, Charles Hockett (1977) neatly divides all instances of word play into two broad categories using terminology normally reserved for literature: *prosaic* and *poetic*. According to Hockett, while prosaic jokes play on some aspect or other of world knowledge, poetic jokes simply play with the language itself.

Such a distinction at first sight appears to be quite helpful; we simply separate jokes containing puns from those that do not:

J9
'Mummy, Mummy, I don't like Daddy!'
'Then leave him on the side of your plate and eat your vegetables.'

J10
Is the tomb of Karl Marx just another Communist plot?

According to Hockett, if we translated J9 into another language it should create no particular linguistic difficulties, while it would be seen as a joke by members of all cultures who share the same eating habits as the British. On the other hand, J10 qualifies for the poetic category owing to the fact that, like the poet, the punster is utilizing an option within the language with which to create an effect. In this case the desired effect is humorous. Undoubtedly, Hockett's distinction is neat and convenient, but it is not completely convincing. The word *plot* does indeed contain an element of duplicity: it is in fact polysemous and an added similarity with poetry is created by the fact that the option played upon (in this case *plot*) is only typical of the source language. It thus follows that poetic jokes tend to encounter similar difficulties to poetry when an attempt is made at translation. Yet to agree with Hockett that a joke such as J9 does not play on language, and merely works on the principle of defeated expectations, would be grossly oversimplifying matters. Although no actual punning (in the traditional sense which sees a pun as a *double entendre*) is involved, the reply forces the recipient to recontextualize the first utterance and in particular the reference of the item *like*. It seems to be a contradiction in terms to suggest that a verbal conceit such as the joke does not in some way play on words. After all, doesn't J9 play on apparently hidden facets of meaning of the item *like*, albeit in a less obvious way than in J10 in which the polysemous item *plot* is exploited.

So any joke, whether it contains a pun or not, by the very nature of its verbalization, necessarily plays on language. It may not be an ambiguous item which acts as its focal point; it could be its delivery, the intonation or the accent in which it is delivered, or even non-verbal additions such as gesture or mime.

At this point, it may be worth commenting on the concept of appreciation of word play. As we have already mentioned, not everybody is amused by the same things and, what is more, over and above shared knowledge of whatever type, finding something funny relies on a number of subjective variables. What may appear amusing under the influence of a few drinks may not appear quite so funny in the cold light of the morning after. A homosexual is hardly going to enjoy being insulted by someone's idea of a witty remark at his or her expense, any more than the Irish are amused by the thousands of jokes which depict them as imbeciles. Some people are offended by sexual innuendo, while others by political references contained in a joke.

Despite our good sense, when someone does not find something funny we often tend to make a character judgement in negative terms. Accusing someone of not having a sense of humour is actually

2   Inside word play

If a group of people were to be asked what they understood by the term 'word play', it would be pretty safe to say that most of them would answer in terms of jokes and puns. What springs to the mind of most people is probably a picture of someone telling a joke or interrupting a conversation with a witty aside or a pun. Quite often, word play is not necessarily a deliberate occurrence. It is perfectly possible to make people laugh quite unintentionally by simply mis-saying something. Someone slips up, says something wrong, and others, for some reason, find this terribly funny. Suddenly we find ourselves faced with an underdog, someone who has slipped up, and who has thus temporarily become our inferior. This, in itself, is funny.

Our present concern is the mistake itself rather than the mechanisms it triggers off at a social level, and, interestingly enough, the kinds of 'mistakes' which people make, and consequently cause others to laugh, appear to be universals in natural languages. As we shall see, languages seem to contain hidden traps at all levels of linguistic analysis, so that a transposed sound or syllable or a misplaced preposition can potentially cause havoc to the general meaning of an utterance. Such havoc provokes laughter.

SLIPS OF THE TONGUE

Slips of the tongue could well be defined as verbal banana skins which cause us, from a position of non-involvement, to laugh at the unknowing victim. Freud's work on verbal blunders and their relationship to the subconscious is so well known that these mistakes have come to be popularly referred to as 'Freudian slips'.

The utterance,

E1

I drove with him tête à bête

(Freud, 1976: 57)

according to Freud, is an 'abbreviation' of a stream of thought which is far more complex than the signal which the surface structure seems to convey. In this case, what the speaker actually says is, in fact, a reduction of something like:

I drove with X tête à tête, and X is a stupid ass.

In other words, the utterance reveals a subconscious thought or idea which is then accidentally (or deliberately in the case of jokes proper) modified slightly. According to Freud it is the very fact that the suppressed 'ass' is given a linguistic form through a 't' which is transformed into a 'b' which makes the example a good joke, by subtly revealing feelings which would have otherwise remained hidden. What is more, the slighter the modification is, the better the joke will be.

It is a well-known fact that Freud interpreted slips in relation to hidden feelings of the psyche. The typing error in a letter enquiring about *pubic transport in Naples* might well have caused Freud to comment on the writer's sexuality. Hockett, however, rather than question the writer's libido, would have explained the error purely in linguistic terms, by putting it down to some kind of 'blend' (1967: 913), although in this particular case the mistake was most probably caused by mere cackhandedness. Nevertheless, slips of the pen, typewriter, word processor and tongue are generally considered amusing. Their recipients laugh at the person who slipped up rather than at the mistake which, in itself, is not funny.

Metathesis

One type of verbal slip which is common to all natural languages is technically known as the 'distant metathesis' or, more colloquially, the 'Spoonerism'; this type of lapse is imitated in intentional word play and owes its name to an Oxford don, Dr William Spooner, who allegedly sent down a student uttering, 'You have deliberately tasted two worms and you can leave Oxford on the town drain.' What happened to the unfortunate Dr Spooner was that he transposed the sounds (in this particular example, /w/ and /t/, and /d/ and /t/) contained in two words within his intended utterance. Owing to the fact that the sentence still made some sort of surrealistic sense, despite the phonological confusion, the tradition of the Spoonerism soon became a traditional form of word play in its own right.

Hockett (1967: 923) considers the utterence, 'I fool so feelish', where 'I feel so foolish' had actually been intended. Rejecting any Freudian interpretations, Hockett sees the metathesized utterence as a blend of the ingredients of the intended utterance. Although the item *fool* precedes *feelish*, *fool* may well be a phonological contamination of *feel* by *foolish*. In fact, it is not unusual for speakers to be aware of the slip which they are about to create, as in the following example:

E2
(intended) according to Smith and Trager
(spoken) according to Smayth? – and Trigger

(ibid.)

After having slipped up, the speaker decides to carry the lapse through as a metathesis, as he is aware that by doing so he is being mildly witty. This example is in direct contrast to Freud's example of someone slipping up on the names Freud and Breuer and referring to the 'Freuer–Breudian method'. Freud suggests that the lapse was due to the fact that the speaker was unimpressed by psychoanalysis. Here too, Hockett puts the slips down to a blend created from two names which are habitually used together.

Hockett provides another interesting example of self-awareness, in which, after the two real lapses, the speaker continues metathesizing even further:

E3
This is how we go to Berkland and Oakley? – Erkland and Boakley? – no, Boakland and Erkley? – darn it! Oakland and Berkeley!

The original slip is a reversal of the initial syllables of the intended place names, the second attempt contains a reversal of the initial consonants of the first slip. In the third attempt, the initial syllables of the second try are interchanged; finally a fourth reversal (this time of the third slip) results in the desired 'Oakland and Berkeley'. Hockett suggests that the speaker was aware of the comic effect of the various permutations and thus classes the example as a 'half-witticism'. Needless to say, beyond such examples we find totally deliberate attempts at metathesizing:

J11
I'd rather have a full bottle in front of me than a full frontal lobotomy.

Malapropisms

Another universal slip is the 'Malapropism'. Sheridan's Mrs
Malaprop (*The Rivals*) is famous for her continual attempts at using
inappropriate words in place of ones which resembled them in sound.
This resulted in disastrous effects such as 'arrangement of epitaphs'
for 'arrangement of epithets'. Clearly, Mrs Malaprop tries to use
words with which she is not accustomed, or what Bolinger calls
'uneducated blends', cases of 'higher level coding falling back on
lower level coding' (1968: 239–40).

What proud parents consider to be 'bright' remarks made by their
toddlers, are caused by the same mechanisms as Malapropisms,
although, unlike their adult/literary counterparts, children using 'difficult' words are not trying to be clever. The child overheard saying
'Nice one, Squirrel', on seeing a squirrel in a park in London, had
obviously misunderstood the name *Cyril* in a popular song of the
time, 'Nice one, Cyril', as *Squirrel*, and therefore knew no differently. The adults present on that particular occasion clearly showed
wonder and amusement at the comment and, by doing so, in a certain
sense 'disrupted' the child's previous discourse. In fact she was
immediately silenced as she found herself becoming the centre of
attention. Similarly the reaction caused by a slip in the flow of a
normal, adult conversation will cause a disruption in its flow, whether
the agent is laughter, a comment or a correction of the mistake.

Misplaced words

Both Sacks (1973) and Sherzer (1978) argue that certain slips of the
tongue actually add to, rather than disrupt, discourse cohesion:

E4
The corral's the big joke now – it just doesn't look very stable.

(Sacks, 1973: 135)

E5
*In his search for economic and military aid, Anwar Sadat has not exactly
been greeted by open arms.*

(CBS News Report, 10 June 1975; Sherzer 1978: 338)

Quick-witted recipients of E4 and E5 will catch on to the unfortunate lexical choices of the two speakers, yet, although discourse may
well be interrupted by a mild chuckle, at the same time those very
choices accentuate cohesion. The recipient with a sense of humour
will misread the adjective *stable* for a noun, thus linking it to *corral*;

the polysemic item *arms* cannot but be linked to *military aid*, thus creating anaphoric indices in both examples. What is more, such cohesion adds to Hockett's argument of linguistic blending. There is no reason why these slips should be considered in terms of the subconscious, when lexical fields might be considered instead. However, cohesive indexing can also be exophoric in nature, as in the following comment by a female poet during a lecture on poetry:

E6
There are some things which only happen to women. Period.
(woman poet reported by Sherzer, 1978)

REPORTED SLIPS

As we have seen, people tend to make mistakes in speech and writing which others are likely to find amusing. Accidental jokes are formally similar to deliberate ones (cf. E3 and J10); the linguistic options available for exploitation to the would-be joker are, of course, limited to the same areas where a potential error may occur. However, before examining the technicalities of deliberate jokes in detail, let us explore briefly an area which lies on the interface between the slip and the joke proper. In the same way as it is perfectly possible to make people laugh by reporting an amusing incident which happened to someone else, we can provoke laughter by simply *reporting* the linguistic mistake made by someone else.

There is a tradition in the British press of reporting instances of unintentional word play in special columns; furthermore, in many newspapers, readers may participate in such columns by sending in examples of lapses they have discovered, in exchange for a modest monetary prize. The more popular press publishes such examples in letter pages, with popular women's magazines specializing in 'bright' remarks made by toddlers.:

E7
My friend's three-year-old son recently made us laugh by pointing out various makes of car, and then asking if ours was a Ford FIASCO!
(H. Gullen, Twickenham; *Woman*, February 14th, 1989)

Bright remarks form a separate category from the bulk of reported slips because of the sort of mechanism which supposedly clicks when the reader sees them. Presumably such clever remarks are considered 'sweet', with the emphasis being very much on the appropriacy of the lapse at such a young age. Nevertheless, let us consider the way the 'joke' is framed. Ms Gullen reports a situation in which she herself, the narrator, is involved. The text leads up to a peak (in this case the punchline) which is couched in terms of a narrative report of a speech act. The next example of a reported gaffe is very different in terms of framing; the 'writer' gives no indication of his amusement regarding what is being reported to his readers, yet he does still create a 'story' around the actual event and consequent slip:

E8

A primary school teacher in Wallington, Oxon. sent a request to a local bookshop for a Diagnostic and Remedial Spelling Manuel and also for a Teacher's Manuel.

(Peterborough Column, *Daily Telegraph*, n.d.)

Here the journalist himself is telling readers about the mistake he has found, with very little elaboration compared to text E7. In fact he limits himself to merely contextualizing the mistake without entering into the story at all. While laughing at the unfortunate Hispanically-influenced teacher, who is unintentionally practising homophony through his/her spelling problems, the reader also laughs with the journalist the self-satisfied laugh of someone who knows better. Let us now compare these examples with texts E9, E10 and E11, where any narrator is totally absent:

E9

It has been medically and scientifically proved that a poet which is properly cared for will keep you active, give comfort and companionship and stimulate comfort and laughter.

(*She*, September 1985)

E10

An American package of a make of contraceptive pill containing two month's supply is labelled 'Twin Pack'.

(*Daily Telegraph*, n.d.)

E11

First Prize in a competition is 'a luxury Caribbean Cruise for two'. Second prize is a rowing machine.

(*Slimming Magazine*)

Here the reader knows the events are being re-told through the context in which they occur. The fact that they appear in columns dedicated to slips of the pen is in itself a pointer for the reader. The reporter simply reports, while it is the macro-frame, the column itself, together with any details which may follow (e.g. E9, E11), which act as structures on which to peg the 'story'.

In E9, the accidentally inserted extra letter renders the whole text as appropriate as it would have been simply with the desired item *pet* and hence it is mildly amusing. E10 and E11 are good examples which parallel Sacks' and Sherzer's examples, E4 and E5, with the difference that, here, the journalist is telling the public what he has read. Anaphoric cohesive irony is displayed in both cases even though *twin* and *rowing machine* are in juxtaposition to the items to which they refer. *Contraceptive pill/twin, cruise/rowing machine* occur in the same respective lexical fields – albeit at opposite poles. The fact that E11 appeared in *Slimming Magazine* adds to the overall irony.

The reader, however, supposedly laughs both *at* the authors of the mistakes and, at the same time, *with* the person who spotted them. The columns which publish these lapses must be prizing the reporters for their powers of observation rather than the cleverness (or funniness) of the remarks themselves.

E12
Sign displayed in shop window: 'Sausages made without conservatives.'

In yet another example from the *Daily Telegraph*, the journalist sets out to make his readers giggle at the thought of eating Tory-flavoured sausages. Despite the spartan frame, the finder of E12 is, in a way, telling a joke. However, the laugh this time is actually on the journalist who is unaware of the double-take which has occurred. It is highly likely that the butcher displaying the sign is a speaker of a Romance language. In Italian, for example, *conservanti* are preservatives and *preservativi* are condoms. It would appear that the butcher in question may have wanted to avoid the use of the word 'preservatives' just in case it had any taboo connotation in English.

Another way of making a joke out of someone else's errors lies in the tradition in such columns of poking fun at hoteliers and caterers the world over in their poor attempts at translating into English; once again we laugh with the discoverer of the gaffes:

E13
In hotel restaurant: 'The waitress will give you the bill and you may sign her on the backside.'

E14
On the coffee shop menu of the excellent Rincombe Hotel in Chiang Mai, Northern Thailand, a recent tourist noted: 'Today's special: Fried crispy wanton with beef and vegetables.'

Here, of course, the reporters distance themselves from the content of what they are reporting by use of quotation marks; they merely set the scene of where the slip occurred and then quote it. This way of structuring verbal blunders can be considered in direct parallel to the ways of framing jokes proper in which a joke might be preceded by something like: 'Have you heard the one about . . .'

I will now report an example of my own of a bad translation which I found on a packet of depilatory wax bought in Italy – it is, however, worth bearing in mind that, while I am presenting it quite crudely, a journalist might well have pre-empted it, or rather framed it, with something like 'Instructions on depilatory wax carton':

E15
Melt wax, shaking from time to time. Then let it make cold somewhat up to reach a certain thickness and make sure the temperature is not extreme. Strew the part to be removed with talcum powder and spread on it a layer of wax longer and larger and of a certain thickness (3 M.M. abt.) so that ot may possible to get hold of it for pulling up. Hardly before wax is solified, take off from skin an end of hair-removing strip so that the same may be kept with safety. As soon as the wax is made cold, get hold of the prearranged end and pull up SUDDENLY. If wisher, apply some cream or oil. Eventual residue of wax are removed passing a cotton flock imbued with alcohol or oil. To removing the hair from the upper lip see the drawings.

Why this should be funny is hard to say. Certainly several syntactic structures have been blatantly misused; yet, rather than laugh at the translator, in this particular case, it is the text itself which triggers off hilarity. It is an obvious word-for-word translation carried out by substituting each source word with the first English equivalent listed in the dictionary without paying attention to target-language word-order. Inappropriate abbreviations and odd use of upper case, together with the alternation of formal items with colloquial terms help create the text's overall comic effect.

DELIBERATE WORD PLAY

Deliberate jokes very often have an 'accidental-but-on-purpose' fla-vour about them. A colleague who insists on calling a textbook 'English *trough* Reading' as opposed to 'English *through* Reading' clearly voices his feelings about the book by means of playing with the spelling, and consequently the pronunciation, of the item *through*. Omitting the first 'h' in that particular word seems to be a mistake which could feasibly be made when writing quickly or per-haps by a non-native speaker. What the 'joker' does is to manipulate the language in such a way that it almost appears to be a slip. In fact, the pseudo-book title could indeed easily be a slip. The difference between the two versions lies only in the fact that, while the deliberate joke sets out as an attempt at being funny, the slip happens to be so fortuitously.

We could go as far as saying that there are two points which match in slips and jokes proper: linguistic form and the underlying stimulus or purpose of the amusing utterance. In his work on the subject of jokes, Freud suggests that deliberate jokes reveal attitudes from the speaker's subconscious in the same way as accidental slips. With both form and stimulus being so similar, we can now see why it is so simple to offend someone because of (what the speaker seems to think is) an innocent joke or remark made in jest. How often is a gaffe followed by a penitent 'I was only joking' on the part of its inventor? The creator of 'English trough Reading' would have to be wary of the company in which he uses his own particular title; nevertheless, should it slip out in the presence of the author, say, he could easily pretend it was just a slip of the tongue.

What now follows is a taxonomy of the different types of language play adopted in deliberate jokes, bearing in mind their direct parallel to so-called Freudian slips. Each subsection contains jokes which exploit a certain linguistic option and is duly classified according to the labels normally used in descriptive linguistics, e.g. graphology, phonology, morphology, lexis, syntax, etc. Wherever possible, examples have been chosen not only because of their resemblance to slips or because they really could have been mistakes, but above all because their authors have done their best to make them appear to be so.

From icon to word

Before considering jokes which are purely verbal, let us briefly consider those which come about by some kind of non-verbal means. There is a whole category of graffiti which is purely iconic. The 'reader' is faced with some kind of diagram which may or may not contain a linguistic sign such as a letter, a number or a word. The following, strictly visual examples were popular amongst servicemen in the early 1960s.

E16

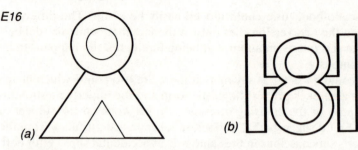

(a)   (b)

The reader is forced to translate these mysterious visual clues into words. In fact, (a) represents 'discontent' (i.e. disc-on-tent) and (b) represents 'hate' (i.e. H + eight = hate). We could say that these illustrations are no more than rebuses which require solving by the reader, yet the links between icon and verbal message are extremely tenuous and it would be rather hard for the reader to actually solve them unless she/he has seen them before. In this sense, these diagrams are reminiscent of riddles which are equally impossible to solve . Both of these verbal and visual riddles are unsolvable; sooner or later the recipient must be given the answer. Nevertheless, they reveal some kind of irritating cleverness on the part of their authors; even without finding these examples funny or particularly clever, recipients are able to recognize that their authors are trying to be so.

Luckily not all graffiti are as difficult to 'solve' as E16. The reader is sometimes given some verbal help from graffitists who couple their diagrams with a caption:

E17

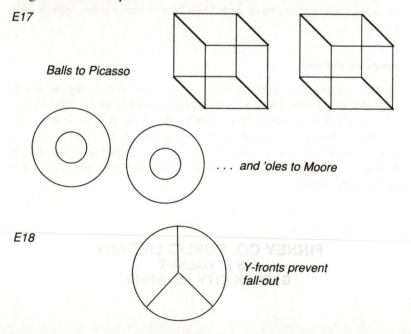

Balls to Picasso

. . . and 'oles to Moore

E18

Y-fronts prevent fall-out

The reader is helped along by the added words, and one could argue that, with an enormous dose of imagination, the two icons in E16 could be 'worked out'; E17 and E18 need their captions to make any sort of sense, as well as knowledge of the intertextual referents (i.e. modern art, CND, men's underwear). There are, however, other graffiti which depend on a less iconic visual element for their impact:

E19

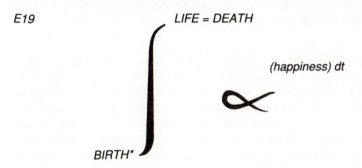

* Life is an integral function of happiness over the time between birth and death.

Here, for the benefit of non-mathematicians, the author provides readers with the solution.

All the examples quoted so far contain a quizzical element; an information gap exists between the graffitist and the reader who has to solve the problem the graffito poses. In this sense, as we have already said, it would appear that these graffiti are closely related to rebuses. They are, in fact, genuine word *games*, literal examples of word *play* which exploit unusual representations of words through a mixture of icons and letters:

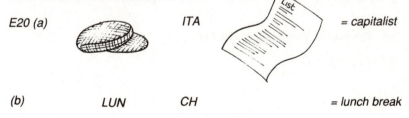

Play need not necessarily involve laughter. The rebuses are not meant to be funny at all but only 'clever', even if many people would agree that they tend to be so in an exasperating way.

Playing with graphology

Verbal graffiti offer us some excellent examples of imitations of genuine spelling mistakes. Consider the similarity between the reported:

E21
Without primeval pants, he argued, we'd still have carbon dioxide of around 15%, instead of the present trace quantity.

(*She*, n.d.)

and a notice in St Mary's church, Oxford, pointing towards the *Brass Rubbing Centre*, which someone has amended to *ass Rubbing Centre* by visibly crossing out the 'B' and the 'r'. Similarly, a graffito declaring *Lesbians – when only the best will do* was changed by inserting an 'r' in 'best' to form 'brest'. The joker tampers with serious written language in a way which is not immediately obvious, yet which, at the same time, reflects some kind of unseen trap inherent in the original text, like the possibility in the example below of inserting an adjective between the participle and the gerund:

E22
PEOPLE HAVE BEEN CROSSING THE CHANNEL TO BOULOGNE FOR YEARS

(with SICK inserted before CROSSING)

(Poster, Waterloo Station, London)

The graffitists of the first two examples have created jokes which could just have easily been mistakes (cf. *pubic transport*, p. 18), yet they are clearly not mistakes. In fact each graffitist has made a point of drawing attention to the amendment.

Hockett's claim that certain jokes can be defined as being *poetic*, finds at least one justification in 'concrete poetry style' graffiti:

E23
(a) *The king of Siam rules Bangk OK[1]*

(b) *Yo-yos rule O –*
                  –
                  –
                  –
                  K

Both these examples need to be seen in order to make any sort of sense at all. It would be extremely difficult, or even impossible, to read them aloud and have them make any sense, let alone render the desired effect. It is hard to imagine what kind of articulatory acrobatics a reading of the 'yo-yo' graffito would involve; similarly a verbalization of E23 (a) could in no way capture the punning of *Bangk OK*.

Of course, poetry should normally be read aloud if we really want to appreciate a text to the full. Many poems depend on devices such as rhyme, rhythm and alliteration, and can only be done justice if read aloud. On the other hand a recital of a poem such as Lewis Carroll's 'Mouse's Tail' would require an extraordinary amount of effort and imagination to illustrate the shape of an ever diminishing tail merely with the use of one's voice.

E24

```
              " Fury said to a
                mouse, That he
             met in the
          house,
       ' Let us
     both go to
      law: I will
          prosecute
            you. Come,
              I'll take no
                denial; We
               must have a
              trial: For
             really this
          morning I've
         nothing
        to do.'
          Said the
            mouse to the
              cur, ' Such
                a trial,
                  dear Sir,
              '       With
                  no jury
                or judge,
               would be
             wasting
            our
             breath.'
               ' I'll be
                a judge, I'll
                  be jury,'
                    said
                  cunning
                 old Fury:
               ' I'll
                try the
                 whole
                   cause
                     and
                   condemn
                  you
               to
                 death.' "
```

Lewis Carroll may well be the inspiration of several joker/poets; consider the technique adopted in the following traditional graffiti and their similarity to *Jabberwocky*:

E25 (a)

IS THIS MIRO WRITING ?

E25 *(b)*

ꙅ'ᗡ⅃ᴚOW   ƎHT   ꙅI   ꙅIHT

ꓶƎⅬIOT   HᴑႱOᴚHT−ƎƎꙅ   TꙄᴚIꟻ

The parallel with poetry can now be taken one step further. Part of the skill involved in 'getting' E23 (a) and (b) lies in knowing that they are indeed 'OK' jokes (naturally, this category of jokes also plays on other devices besides graphology). The reader needs to recognize that they belong to a certain genre, and to understand what the genre is. It is not sufficient merely to link Siam and Bangkok or know what to do with a yo-yo.

The OK form of late twentieth-century 'laymen's poetry' has established its own forms and traditions to which all its poets must adhere. In order to invent an OK graffito the writer has to be able to imitate the form, structure and rhythm of all the other graffitists of the school who have gone before him/her. As with 'real' poets, any one of them may break the tradition and start off a new school. If a new formula catches on, then a new tradition (and school) will flourish in its own right. So, returning to examples E23 (a) and (b), we can now see that the reader must be capable of recognizing that the writer has manoeuvred the formula 'X Rules OK' to accommodate a link with Siam or a yo-yo.

Furthermore, let us not forget the considerable difficulty involved in translating such poetry/graffiti into another language. After all, what likelihood is there of, for example, *Miró* (/mɪrə/) having a mispronounced homophonic counterpart in Russian or Spanish?

Anagrams

E26
Anagrams rule – or Luke?

As every crossword addict knows, *or Luke* is a signal that the utterance is in a cryptic code which requires unravelling by the reader. The OK genre has now been twisted to accommodate the mental scrabble of the anagram.

E27
Alas poor Yorlik, I knew him backwards

Traditionally, anagrams are warped signifiers which warn their recipients that they contain a buried signified which wants to surface. It is the word *backwards* which tells the recipient how to unpuzzle the anagram by reading something in the utterance from left to right. The joke is, of course, doubly intertextual. Apart from the clear Shakespearian reference, *Yorlik* backwards reads *Kilroy*, the well-known character who is frequently mentioned in the slogan *Kilroy was here*. Yet again the recipient is faced with having to know about an item of world knowledge which is imperative for the complete appreciation of the joke.

E28
Say it with Fowler's
(sign above dictionaries in London bookshop)

E28 can also be read at more levels. It is not a true anagram at all, because Fowler is indeed the editor of the dictionary in question. However, a rearrangement of the letters of the editor's name will produce the item *flowers* and hence the Interflora slogan, *Say it with flowers*. The 'joke' is obviously more enjoyable if the reader can appreciate it on both levels.

Palindromes

For the sake of completeness, I should like to briefly mention palindromes, words which read in both directions. The phrase *Madam, I'm Adam* has a nonsensical appeal to it which is quite inexplicable, and British schoolchildren continue to savour the traditional 'naughtiness' of *Was it Eliot's toilet I saw?*

Playing with sounds

As Opie and Opie point out (1959), word play is first learnt in the playground, with tongue-twisters certainly being one of a child's first encounters with it. The acoustic complexity of *Peter Piper's pickled pepper* is pleasing to the ear, and its performance involves a challenge. Furthermore, when someone slips up in trying to utter a tongue-twister, matters become even more amusing to whoever is listening. As was pointed out earlier, people tend to laugh at others' misfortunes, and schoolchildren find out pretty quickly that if they can trap a chum into saying something wrong, they will then (a) feel good and (b) look clever in front of their friends. If whatever is said also happens to be 'naughty', then the instigator gains even more points. A phrase like *The elephant is sitting on the bucket* can be transformed into something totally unintelligible if someone is made to utter it

with their forefingers stretching their lips to their outmost limits –
unintelligible except for the words *fuck it*, the naughtiness of which is
bound to provoke peals of laughter in anyone of primary school age.

As we saw previously (see p. 18), the Spoonerism originated as a
slip of the tongue which developed into a deliberate joking convention. Due to the fact that nowadays this form of word play has a
tendency to be somewhat obscene, traditionally, the taboo part of the
utterance is usually left for the recipient to complete mentally:

J12
Q. What's the difference between a Radox bath and Louis Frémaux?
A.   Radox bucks up the feet.

The answer is of course incomplete and presents the recipient with an
interesting challenge. However, the recipient must recognize that the
answer is indeed incomplete; native speakers automatically recognize
this as they possess prior knowledge of the fact that they will be
required to transpose certain syllables in order to obtain the 'answer'.
The recipient may well be aware that Radox are bath salts but will not
necessarily know at the outset that Louis Frémaux is a conductor.
While the native speaker will be able to work this out by transposing
the 'f' and the 'b' in the answer, a foreigner will surely remain
nonplussed. The native speaker knows that the unanswerable question itself indicates the onset of a joke. Children's riddles frequently
play on this very type of metathesis. Two totally different elements
are put up for comparison:

J13
Q. What's the difference between a doormat and a bottle of medicine?

A less than serious answer is expected because of the nonsensical
nature of the question itself. There are, of course, dozens of differences between doormats and medicine, just as there are between bath
salts and conductors of orchestras. The absurd question is itself an
indicator that we are in the field of humorous discourse.

A.   One's taken up and shaken and the other's shaken up and taken.

The recipient clearly knows what to expect; if in his/her childhood the
answer to such questions involved a common denominator which
consisted of a symmetrical transposition of initial word sounds, then
it must surely follow that if *Radox bucks up the feet . . .* then *Frémaux
fucks up the beat*.

The kind of knowledge required to get these Spoonerisms is quite
complex. What chance would a non-native speaker have of 'getting'
the following example:

J14
I'm ash nished as a pewt.

Even if they were *au fait* with the idiom *to be as pissed as a newt,* will they also see the cleverness of the added /ʃ/ sound? In other words do drunkards slur their 's's universally?

The transposition of sounds/syllables can occur anywhere within a word, as in the amendment to a name plate on a Paolozzi sculpture at Euston station, where 'Piscator' is transformed into *Pis-tacor.* Somehow, the recipient must know that the joker requires them to make a mental somersault and pronounce it /telkər/ as opposed to /taːkor/. Here too knowledge of all three subsystems (see p. 13) is required.

Manoeuvring phonology

One step further from play on individual sounds, we find play on supra-segmental features such as stress:

J15
Q. How do you make a cat drink?
A. Easy, put it in a liquidizer.

J16
I thought Wanking was a town in China until I discovered Smirnoff.

The rather cruel riddle of J15 demonstrates that by giving prominence to the item *drink* ('cat DRINK') the recipient is led to imagine that the answer will have something to do with ways of feeding a feline. By switching the prominence to 'CAT drink', the riddler invents a rather nasty cocktail.

In slightly more technical terms, we could say that an axial clash has occurred. In the question the item *cat* is a noun and *drink* is a verb, while in the answer the two items are interpreted as a single item, a compound noun *cat drink*:

             ↗LION
(a) How do you make a CAT drink?
             ↘DOG

(b) How do you make a CATDRINK?
               MILKSHAKE?
               COCKTAIL?

In J16 we see that prominence can also be spread differently within a more complex lexical item. The reader – *reader* rather than listener because this example aims at tricking the recipient into misreading what would be otherwise disambiguated if heard – will understand 'WanKING' mainly because of the misleading upper case 'W'. Only on reflection will he/she realize that the referent is a verbal participle and not a proper noun. In other words, according to the versions we wish to accept, the items in the first half of the riddle and the first syllable of *wanking* occupy different slots along the syntagmatic axis. When the wrong filler (accidentally or otherwise) is placed in the wrong slot, the paradigmatic invades the syntagmatic. Unlikely items invade territory which is not normally theirs. Joel Sherzer defines a pun as 'a projection of the paradigmatic onto the syntagmatic' (Sherzer, 1978: 341), thus rejecting the common interpretation of a pun as a word with two meanings.

In this light puns are seen as items which occur outside their expected habitat. Sherzer goes on to add that such an interpretation of a pun is 'precisely the Jakobsonian definition of poetry'. We can now, perhaps, consider the link between this and Hockett's definition of jokes as 'layman's poetry'. As we saw previously, Hockett argues that, like the poet, the punster has a variety of options within the language at his or her disposal with which to create a certain effect. The fact that poetry presents greater difficulty than prose in translation is one of Hockett's strongest arguments in his pun = poem equation. However, so-called *prosaic* jokes, with heavy culture-specific content, present the translator with equally complex problems. While it is undeniable that poetry exploits linguistic features inherent in a language – sometimes to the point of exasperation, as in concrete poetry, for example – to imply that the opposite is true of prose (and consequently of prosaic jokes) is somewhat oversimplifying matters. Hockett's definition of poetry thus finds itself in opposition to Jakobson's, which is not confined to 'high flown' poetry alone (and consequently seen in terms of features such as alliteration, paranomasia, dactyl metre and so forth), but also includes occurrences in the referential function. Prose itself is thus seen as a continuum in which the referential function and the poetic function are intertwined to varying degrees, with 'literary' prose closer to the 'poetic' end of the cline than 'practical' prose. As jokes are examples of the creative use of language which breaks pre-established patterns of clearly referential prose, in Jakobsonian terms, any joke by definition is poetic whether linguistically or socioculturally inclined.

Playing with word boundaries

Many jokes create axial clashes by generating more than one item from what was a single item in the first place by means of the elimination of original word boundaries.

J17
Knock knock . . .
Who's there?
Felix
Felix who?
Felix-ited all over!
(Feel excited all over)

Needless to say, the joker is doubly cheating the recipient as he/she is combining the formation of new boundaries with a form of distant homophony. Stretching the name *Felix* to *feel excited*, while showing considerable imagination, at the same time appears incongruous in the environment of the joke as a whole and thus results in being irritating rather than funny. This type of play is a traditional children's favourite; let us consider 'Batty Book Titles':

J18
Keep Fit by Jim Nastics
Keep it Up by Lucy Lastic
Victorian Transport by Orson Cart
Hospitality by Collin Anytime
The Arthur Negus Story by Anne Teaks

(School Magazine, 1970)

What takes place in these examples is that first the joker thinks of a word within the same lexical field as the book title and then extracts a name from it. This name should, of course, be linked in some way to the subject matter of the title. For example *Jim Nastics*, two items which are easily extracted from the single item *gymnastics*, provide a fitting author for a book on keeping fit; just as *Anne Teaks* aptly authors a book about a popular antique dealer, and so on. Of course, all such examples cross-cut two word-play techniques by exploiting homophony (or, at least, a distant type of homophony, see p. 38) and word boundaries at the same time.

The tendency in English to link words together to form a single stream of sound, a single phonological word, lends itself perfectly to this type of play:

J19
BE ALERT!
Your country needs lerts!

This classic graffito commonly found scrawled beneath wartime posters transforms the adjective *alert* into the determiner *a* + nonce noun *lert*. Here too we can consider these examples in terms of axial clashes. Unlike J15 and J16 where whole words invade syntagmatic slots which in 'normal' contexts would be reserved for different choices, in J17, J18 and J19 the reverse happens as entire words aredeconstructed to accommodate more syntagmatic slots. Any adjective beginning with 'a' could thus be expanded in the same way:

Don't be afraid! Your country doesn't need fraids!

Of course deconstructions are often more complex. Consider the transformation of transcendental meditation in the following aside:

J20
Is a Buddhist monk refusing an injection at the dentist's trying to transcend dental medication?

The adjective *transcendental* 'contains' the verb *transcend* and the adjective *dental*. The author has to create a situation which is apt for both a monk and dentistry. By changing *meditation* to *medication*, he/she is able to transfer the monk to the dentist's surgery and can thus create a situation in which he/she can toy with the two new words.

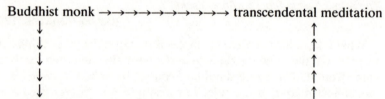

Playing with word formation

A common game amongst children is for one child to ask: 'What's a baby pig called?' The response is of course 'piglet'. 'So, what's a baby toy called?' and the stooge says 'toilet'. As in the 'Knock knock' joke, the recipient is deliberately set up to fall into a linguistic trap, which in this particular case consists of saying something 'rude'.

Another interesting example of pseudo-English morphology is provided by the Goons' classic exchange:

J21
Seagoon: A penguin please.
Sellers: Certainly, I'll look in the catalogue.
Seagoon: But I don't want a cat, I want a penguin!
Sellers: Then I'll look in the penguin-logue.

Of course, correct morphology can be exploited too, like in one-liners such as:

J22
Genius is 1% inspiration and 99% perspiration.

Somehow, however, 'silly', pseudo morphology is more appealing:

J23
If Typhoo puts the 'T' in Britain, who puts the 'arse' in Marseilles?

There is no answer because the fact that *tea* happens to be a homophone of a letter of the alphabet, does not form a symmetrical whole with the combination of letters which form the word *arse*.

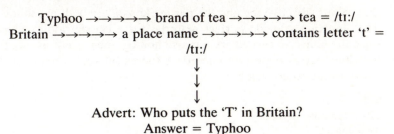

Typhoo →→→→→→ brand of tea →→→→→→ tea = /tiː/
Britain →→→→→→ a place name →→→→→→ contains letter 't' = /tiː/

↓
↓
↓

Advert: Who puts the 'T' in Britain?
Answer = Typhoo

Similarly:
Marseilles →→→→→→ a place name →→→→→→ contains word 'arse'
'arse' = ø

↓
↓
↓

∴ Who puts the 'arse' in Marseilles?
Answer = ?

Playing with lexis

Three closely related word-play options, which are however quite distinct, are: homophones (words which sound the same but have different meanings); homonyms (words with the same form but with different meanings); and polysemes (single words with different meanings). The similarity of these options lies in the duplicity each one possesses which is inherent in the language itself. This quality is absent in the comic options examined so far in which the joker has had to intervene in some way with the item which is at the focus or punch of the joke. As we have seen in the examples, word boundaries needed to be tampered with or syllables manoeuvred from outside the text in order to imitate a slip. When it comes to lexical play using the options mentioned above, the joker has simply to find an environment in which to place an item which is already two-faced in its own right. In other words, rather than render an item ambiguous by meddling with the item itself, it is the situation around the item which has to be adapted to contain the duplicity already inherent in the focus item.

Homophones

J24
Q.   *What's black and white and red all over?*
A.   *A newspaper.*

The colour adjective *red* and the participle *read* are both pronounced /red/ and thus provide perfect material for a classic riddle, which, since the items concerned are not also homographs, is not as successful when read as opposed to heard. A successful adult version of the above riddle could well be:

J25
The three ages of man:
Tri-weekly
Try weekly
Try weakly

Homophones in jokes and quips are not, however, always pure in nature. Very often, in fact, homophony is merely alluded to:

J26
All men eat but Fu Manchu.

Fu Manchu can vaguely sound like 'few men chew' when set beside *all men eat*. The aside is neat, the word groups on either side of *but* contain the same number of syllables and mirror each other lexically: *all/few, men/man, eat/chew*. In more technical terms, such distant or allusive homophony is known as *alliteratio*;[2] two 'words' in which the beginning and/or the end are phonetically the same. Needless to say, in this example, word boundaries have also been disrupted.

Allusive homophony may also be a combination of *alliteratio* with the *homeoteleuton*, a word in which the substitution of one or more syllables for another occurs:

J27
Are eskimos God's frozen people?

These two techniques occur in 'bilingual' puns, although the sounds alluded to are anglicized versions of the 'foreign' sound. Copywriters working on the Perrier mineral water advertising campaign have successfully exploited the tendency of English speakers to pronounce the word *eau* /əʊ/, in slogans such as *Who put the 'eau' in bottles?*, *Eau-la-la* and *Picasseau*, below a cubist version of a Perrier bottle.

J28
Q. *What do Frenchmen have for breakfast?*
A. *Huit-heures-bix! (Weetabix)*

This children's riddle combines (a) a French (supposedly) pronunciation of a popular breakfast cereal, which (b) in a French accent just happens to mean 'eight o'clock', with (c) a common tendency in some regions of Britain to insert an /r/ after the /ə/ in the item *Weetabix*.

French is not the only target for bilingual punners:

J29
Amo, amas, amatit again.

Homonyms and polysemes

The distinction between homonymy and polysemy is extremely subtle. Leech quite rightly asks himself:

> Why should we decide that there are two separate nouns 'mole' rather than two separate meanings of the same word?
>
> (Leech, 1969)

However, as was pointed out previously, puns (whether phonetic or semantic) are two-faced. Their hidden meaning is brought out by the environment in which they occur, where a more 'obvious' meaning is usually expected.

J30
There was a record number of births in Kilburn this week. Apparently, it was due to the Irish sweep. He has now moved to Camden town.
> (*The Two Ronnies*)

The item *sweep* is a homonym. At first sight, it appears to mean 'raffle' or 'lottery', but as we read on and the text unravels, we see that the meaning 'chimney sweep' is intended instead. Although the surprise pronoun *he* on the one hand disrupts the text, on the other hand it also adds to its overall cohesion in the same way as the

unintentional lexical slips presented by Sacks and Sherzer do (E4 and
E5). However, ambiguity which depends on polysemy is more subtle
than homonymic play:

J31
Bloodnok: You can't come in, I'm in the bath.
Seagoon: (off) What are you doing in the bath?
Bloodnok: I'm watching television.
Seagoon: (off) What's showing?
Bloodnok: My dear fellow – nothing. I've got a towel round me.

(*The Goon Show*)

In contrast to the item *sweep* which can represent two separate lexical
words, the item *showing* is one word which can have more meanings.
In this case, Seagoon's question in which he wants to know what is
showing on television is deliberately misinterpreted by Bloodnok as
wanting to know which parts of his anatomy are showing. The
openendedness of the following graffito leads jokers to generate
several jokes:

J32
Jesus saves!

(sign outside church)

– with the Woolwich!
– he couldn't do it on my salary!
– but Bremner scores on penalty!
– Green Shield stamps!
– he's a redeemer too!

(graffiti below)

While being lexical in nature, the type of play exploited verges on the
syntactic as the item *save* occurs without an object, thus paving the
way for manipulation. The final polysemic reference to *redeeming*
generates from both *Jesus* and *Green Shield stamps*.

Playing with syntax

J33
A Scotsman takes all his money out of the bank once a year for a holiday;
once it's had a holiday he puts it back again.

J34
Child: Mummy, can I go out to play?
Mother: With those holes in your trousers?
Child: No, with the girl next door.

Both examples play on an ambiguity which can easily occur in the English language when sentences contain rank-shifted prepositional-groups. In J33 the group *for a holiday* could refer back to both *the Scotsman* and *his money*. The recipient's common sense will naturally lead him/her to suppose that Scotsmen go on holiday rather than sums of money. However expectations are defeated when presented with the subject *it* in the second half of the sentence. The same thing occurs in J34 when the child misinterprets the prepositional opening with the item *with*. Rank-shifted prepositionals in the nominal group can only be disambiguated by examining their deep structure. By modifying J33 to something like '. . . once a year so that he can go on holiday . . .', and J34 to 'Wearing those trousers with holes in?', any ambiguity would be avoided. However, although this would indeed create a more economical form, it would do so at the expense of a potential joke.

J35

Trimmets treacle puddings have caused several people to be taken to hospital with badly scalded feet. It seems that the instructions read: 'Open tin and stand in boiling water for twenty minutes.'

Ambiguity is caused by the absence of an object after the verb *stand*, further strengthened by the absence of a specific subject in the imperative form.

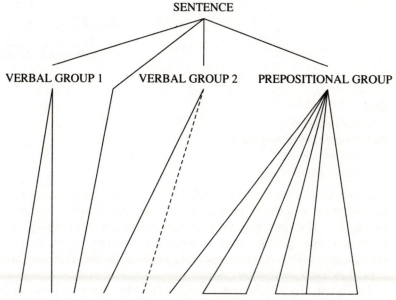

SENTENCE

VERBAL GROUP 1   VERBAL GROUP 2   PREPOSITIONAL GROUP

'Open   tin   and   stand   [tin ∅]   in   boiling   water   for   twenty   minutes.'

Such a joke must surely be a descendant of the traditional 'gaffe' seen in church halls:

Ladies are asked to rinse out teapots and stand upside down in the sink.

Once again the subject of the second imperative is missing together with its object; an examination of the sentence's deep structure is necessary in order to disambiguate it:

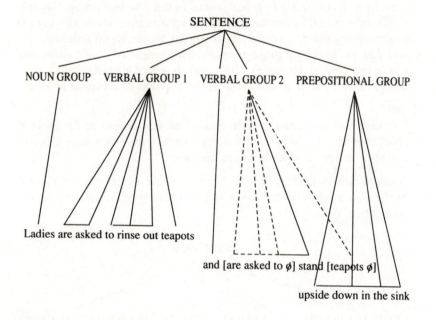

J36
Advertising slogan:
Nothing acts faster than Anadin
Traditional response:
Then take nothing!

The fact that items like 'nothing', 'nobody', etc. do not need to be preceded by a negative particle when they act as subjects, creates ambiguity. 'Nothing' may thus become a name for 'something' as it gains tangible qualities and materially exists due to its syntactic positioning. Following this logic, *take nothing* can therefore be interpreted as 'take something'.

The ambiguity of the indefinite article which can be used as an indicator of both specific reference and generic reference can also be exploited for humorous ends:

J37
During a statistics lesson, the teacher says:
'In Tokyo a man gets run over every five hours.'
'Oh, poor thing!' remarks a pupil.

Playing with the rules of conversation

As we have seen so far, in order to play with language, there must be something linguistically ambiguous about the text, or else the joker has in some way to render it so. We have seen how features such as sounds, words, parts of words and even syntactic structures can all become two-faced; yet over and above the traditional hierarchy of the language system (i.e. graphology, phonology, morphology, lexis and syntax) lies a supra-structure, pragmatics, which can be as ambiguous as a discrete item. Choices and restrictions which a language user encounters in conversation can become two-faced when seen in relation to form.

J38
At the customs:
Customs officer: Cigarettes, brandy, whisky . . .
Girl: How kind you are in this country. I'll have a coffee please!

This joke illustrates how form and function may well clash when a single form covers more functions. In this case a request for information is misunderstood to imply an offer.

Conversational markers can be taken literally, rather than the pointers which they are supposed to be:

J39
'You know your great great great great great great grandfather?'
'Yeah?'
'No you don't, he's dead!'

The words *you know* are merely indicators which draw attention to something which is about to be said. They stand for something like: 'Hey, I'm going to talk about x . . . are you concentrating on x?' In the following example they are deliberately misinterpreted at face value.

J40
'Oh Nigel, I hear you buried your mother-in-law last week.'
'Had to. She was dead.'

A stock way of introducing a certain subject with the aim of getting the interlocutor to develop it is, here too, interpreted at face value. Instead of talking about the death and funeral of his mother-in-law, discreetly alluded to with *I hear you buried* . . ., the recipient explains why she was buried.

We can now see that the area in which serious discourse ends and humorous discourse begins is not necessarily well defined. At first sight it may appear, for example, that the manipulation of discourse markers can mislead an interlocutor into thinking we are being serious when we are joking or vice versa. In such an example, what is happening is not so much that certain markers (or functions) are simply multifarious, but that Grice's co-operative principles are not being totally respected.

J41
Constantinople is a very long word, can you spell it?

Whether the recipient answers by spelling out 'Constantinople' or 'it', he/she will be wrong because *it* can refer to both *Constantinople* and *it*. Amongst Grice's maxims of manner we find: 'Avoid ambiguity'; so, if I really want someone to spell IT (i.e. the word 'it') and not (the word) CONSTANTINOPLE, I make sure that my intonation is such that inverted commas are clearly heard around the 'it'; this will also stop me from breaking another maxim: 'Avoid obscurity of expression'. What is more, by not being as informative as might perhaps be required, a maxim of quantity is also being broken. As all linguistic play is ambiguous, it follows that all exchanges containing play are deliberately flouting one or more of Grice's principles. Nevertheless, in the field of pragmatic play, rule-breaking is more subtle than in other areas. Another answer to J41 could be an equally uncooperative 'Yes/No', which would counterbalance the ambiguous posit. (Consider also: 'Have you got the time/a light/a cigarette?' 'Yes'.)

J42
Where did King John sign the Magna Carta?

Here the recipient is faced with a question and not unreasonably tries to respond to a request for information by remembering his/her history. However he/she will soon find that no city or town is the right one because King John signed the Magna Carta *at the bottom*. The question is intentionally misleading, not only because of the many-sidedness of the item *where*, but above all because of the insufficient information given (quantity maxim), its obscurity (manner maxim), and its deception (quality maxim). Of course, the sender could equally well have asked 'On which part of the Magna Carta did King John sign his name?', but that would have been playing fair, which, as we have seen, is not always the intention of our interlocutors.

INEXPLICABLE PLAY ON LANGUAGE

Much word play cannot be catalogued according to the traditional labels considered so far, yet, at the same time, does not necessarily play on sociocultural features either.

J43
Kenneth Horne: Do you know anything about Professor Cornposture?
Stooge: Oh, he's the world's leading expert in ballistic missiles; he won last year's Nobel Prize in Physics and he's head of the science department at Yale. Why do you ask?
Kenneth Horne: He asked me to lend him five shillings.

(*Round the Horne*)

Why this short text should be funny is quite baffling. Undoubtedly it can be explained in terms of a let-down of the recipient's expectations; after the build-up regarding the Professor's curriculum, we find that Kenneth Horne merely wants to make sure that if he lends him five shillings he can be certain of getting it back. However, is this really sufficient to trigger off the amount of laughter which this exchange actually manages to achieve? The recording of the programme in which this particular joke occurs contains no canned laughter and yet it raises an enormous amount of authentic laughter. To suggest that it is funny only because the recipient is let down or because western society tends to joke about meanness seems unsatisfactory. On the other hand, it is worth noting that the audience begin giggling as soon as they hear the Professor's surname. Here too, we cannot help but ask ourselves, why should the name *Cornposture* be funny *per se*? Yet it is. Could it be that names containing words pertaining to the lower regions of the body are inherently funny just because they are reminiscent of something 'rude'? The surname 'Higginbottom', for example, is certainly considered funny by some people, as is the inventor of Toad in the Hole, Robert Capability Lackwind (another name which gets a laugh) (*Round the Horne*). Together with diverse aspects connected with 'bottoms', perhaps a reference to feet and consequently 'corns' is funny too.

Other banter can be considered funny because of indirect implications to subject matter outside the text.

J44
Nurse: Have you had any of the diseases on this list?
Hancock: Show me . . . (pause) How dare you! No I have not and especially
not that one!

(Hancock's Half Hour)

The more quick-witted members of the audience laugh at Hancock's
first *How dare you!* They have already caught on to the fact that at
least one of the diseases on the list is venereal, before Hancock gives
them a complete confirmation with his indignation at being suspected
of having *that one*. So, on the one hand, Hancock is playing on the
universal of the sexual innuendo, while, on the other hand, he does
so through oblique allusion and, of course, clever use of timing. Let
us not forget that *Hancock's Half Hour* was originally intended for
radio and that Hancock could only depend on language, without any
visual help, to raise a laugh. In this light, we can now see just how
much of the text depends on the listener's interaction.

J45
The answers to last week's quiz . . . the answer to question one was in three
parts: the three thirty from Paddington, the Wheeltapper's daughter and not
while the train is standing in the station.

(Round the Horne)

What is it that should not be done while the train is standing in the
station? At first the mind boggles, yet we instinctively feel that it must
be something 'naughty'. Then we recall the warnings in lavatories on
trains and find that our instinctive suspicions are confirmed.
However, it is not only the implied reference to toilets which provokes laughter. Surely it is something which is missing from the text,
which is unsaid, that makes us laugh. In fact, the audience begins to
laugh as soon as they hear *the three thirty from Paddington*, and the
laughter increases with the subsequent answers, thus demonstrating
that the idea of a link between the three answers must contain the
source of laughter. What silly, nonsensical links these may be remains
a mystery.

J46
Whenever there's any honi-soiting, there you'll find them mal-y-pensing.

This aside by Kenneth Williams refers to the activities of the board of
censors at the BBC. Once again it is hard to establish exactly why it is
funny. Here, of course, the language has been manipulated, yet it is
probably fair to say that the transformation of the quotation alludes

to something 'naughty'. One possible interpretation could be that *honi-soiting* alludes to some kind of 'carrying on' while *mal-y-pensing* remains a witty anglicization of 'thinking evil'.

NOTES

1 The origins of this genre of graffiti are not very clear. The most probable explanation for it is that it is a direct descendant of the football slogan, *X Rules OK*, where '*X*' stands for the name of a football club, e.g. *Chelsea Rules OK*. From the late 1960s, such slogans have been sprayed on walls throughout the British Isles as the territorial war-cry of a rather violent category of young supporter. It would appear that these slogans were then emulated by graffitists in forms like *Saliva Drools OK*, *Matadors Rule*, *Olé*, etc.

2 These definitions are my own translations of those quoted by Heinrich Lausberg in *Elemente der literarischen Rhetorik*, Munich, Max Hueber Verlag, 1967.

3 Framing word play

Jokes come in numerous shapes and sizes ranging from very long and highly structured 'shaggy dog stories' to short, almost spineless one-liners. Depending on the length of a joke, the recipient's attention may be engaged for several minutes to hear a complex plot unfold before the narrative explodes into a pun, or else she/he may be suddenly surprised by a clever quip casually thrown into an ordinary conversation. Whatever the type of joke, however, for it to qualify as such, what is commonly known as a punchline or a punch must always be present.[1] The punch is the point at which the recipient either hears or sees something which is in some way incongruous with the linguistic or semantic environment in which it occurs but which at first sight had not been apparent. If the incongruity met with appears in the form of a pun, a new and unexpected meaning of the form in question will suddenly become apparent; if it implies a situation, it will be equally new and surprising.

There was an Irishman an Englishman and . . . BANG!!!

The recipient of the above joke expects the words *a Scotsman* to follow the ritualistic opening to what appears to be a classic Irish joke. Instead the punch occurs in an unexpected position thus dashing our expectations. There will be no symmetrical succession of similar events acted out in a similar way by three stereotypical characters. What is more, there will be no incongruity performed by the Irishman which will finally act as a punch. All this is pre-empted by a sort of premature punch in the word *Bang*! The recipient is aware of what sometimes happens in real life when certain Irishmen and Englishmen come together, and the frame of a put-down Irish joke serves as a front to express deeper goings on. Over and above this, however, the joke makes fun of itself by playing with a convention of which the recipient is well aware.

The punch is the pivot around which a joke is centred. Provided that the pragmatic signals telling them that a joke is on its way have been received, recipients expect a punch sooner or later. The Irish joke above is a particularly good one because the recipient does indeed expect a punch much later on than it actually occurs. Now, despite the fact that recipients usually know that a punch is on its way, the joke will still tend to create a certain amount of unexpectedness. Even if the joke is not a particularly good one, the anti-climax of the punch itself will be sufficient to create a feeling of surprise. It is the very mixture of expectancy and surprise which makes up the punchline.

Before going into more depth regarding the breaking or twisting of the unspoken rules of jokes in order to create a better joke, let us see what the rules of a typical or 'normal' joke may be. Let us begin by considering a more predictable Irish joke.

THE JOKE AS A NARRATIVE FORM

There was a Scotsman, an Italian and an Irishman. They wanted to watch the Olympic Games but they didn't have tickets, so they decided to go as athletes.

The Scotsman pulled a bollard out of the ground, put it over his left shoulder, went to the ticket office and said: 'Jock McTavish, Scotland, Caber Tossing.' And in he went.

The Italian found an empty plate, put it under his left arm, went to the ticket office and said: 'Giovanni Bianchi, Italy, Discus Throwing.' And in he went.

The Irishman scratched his head and thought. Then he put some barbed wire under his left arm, went to the ticket office and said: 'Paddy Murphy, Ireland, Fencing.'

Goldilocks would not be quite the same if she had not sat on three chairs, tasted three plates of porridge and lain down on three beds while the Big Bad Wolf had to huff and puff three times over in order to be taken seriously by the three little pigs. Similarly, things in Irish jokes happen in multiples of three. First, the joke needs three characters, who are usually English, Scottish and Irish, but nationality variants, as in the example above, do exist if they are necessary to the plot. Second, the joke typically consists of three symmetrical events in which the three characters mirror each other in some way. Finally, the third event, in which the Irishman is the protagonist will contain an incongruity. The Irishman will do something stupid, something very wrong, and this is the punch of the joke. Everything which has gone before it is merely a build-up for the final resolution.

A common discourse pattern of clause relationships in English is the Problem–Solution pattern. Texts can be seen to hang together according to a surface pattern which can be labelled:

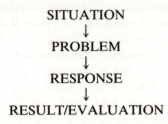

We can easily imagine how different texts ranging from the purely referential to the literary can be analysed according to these criteria. Advertisements, for example, frequently present readers with an explicit problem (which they often never knew they even had), only to be given a solution in the product being advertised. An example of this can be seen in the 1960s advert: 'Headache? Tense, nervous headache? Take Anadin' in which the Situation/Problem/Solution paradigm is resolved in the few words of a brief slogan. Fairy-tales, romantic novels and situation comedies also present the reader/viewer with a problem which is resolved by the end of the tale when we are told or left to presume that the protagonist 'lives happily ever after'. Jokes, like advertising texts, frequently present an explicit problem. Let us see what happens if we analyse our Irish joke from a 'problem/solution' viewpoint (see Figure 1).

The first two episodes act as successful attempts at resolving the initial problem of getting into the stadium:

'Jock McTavish,	'Giovanni Bianchi,
Scotland,	Italy,
Caber tossing.'	Discus throwing.'
And in he went.	And in he went.

The result of the Irishman's actions are not successful and are not verbalized with a matching *And in he went*:

'Paddy Murphy,
Ireland,
Fencing.'

What does or does not happen is simply understood through the pun on the word *fencing*. As it is not spelt out explicitly, the recipient has to work out the underlying implication of the result, partly by linking it back to the caber tossing and the discus throwing mentioned by the other two protagonists. Automatically, and at the same time

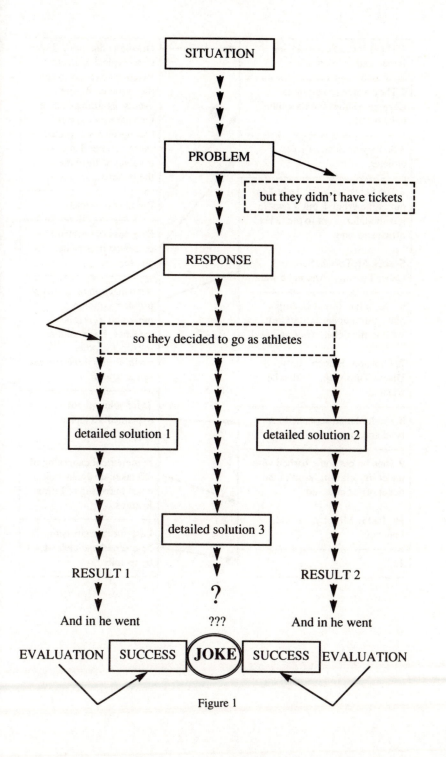

Figure 1

1 There was a Scotsman, an Italian and an Irishman.	Opening containing three stereotypical characters. Recipient expects to hear the narration of three events regarding each of the characters in turn. Incongruity is expected at event number 3 and will involve the third man, i.e. the Irishman.
2 They wanted to go to the Olympic Games but they didn't have tickets.	
3 So they decided to go as athletes.	
4 The Scotsman pulled a bollard out of the ground, put it over his left shoulder, went to the ticket office and said:	Problem presented.
	Response to problem presented in previous clause.
5 'Jock McTavish, Scotland, Caber Tossing.' And in he went.	Verbalization of details of problem/solution presented in second sentence. Each solution mirrors the other rhythmically, lexically and syntactically.
6 The Italian found an empty plate, put it under his left arm, went to the ticket office and said:	
7 'Giovanni Bianchi, Italy, Discus Throwing.' And in he went.	
8 The Irishman scratched his head and thought.	Third solution not explained. Recipient expects punch.
9 Then he put some barbed wire under his left arm, went to the ticket office and said:	Symmetrical patterning of 4/5 taken up again with exact mirroring of formal features.
10 'Paddy Murphy, Ireland, Fencing.'	Last utterance missing. To be inserted and understood by recipient.
11 ?	

silently, the recipient puzzles out the punch. In contrast to the more 'serious' forms of narrative mentioned previously, we could say that joke narrative differs because of what is implicit within the punch. It is this very implication, this cryptic element which differentiates the joke from many other texts. The advertising slogan was obliged explicitly to spell out the solution to a tense, nervous headache. A joke cannot do this. Typically, the text leading up to the punchline is detailed and explicit while multiple meanings are packed into the few words contained in the verbally contracted punch. Our Irish joke could well have finished in the following way:

'Paddy Murphy, Ireland, Fencing.' And he didn't get in because you don't fence with barbed wire, even if it is used for the building of fences.

However this detailed verbalization of the result is, of course, unnecessary and transforms the joke into a non-joke by the very explicitness of the finale. Let us see if the same is true of other 'story'-style jokes by examining another type of joke, the 'Shaggy Dog Story':

Once upon a time there were three rabbits, Foot, Foot-Foot and Foot-Foot-Foot, and they all lived at the bottom of Farmer Brown's garden. (S1)

One day the rabbits were feeling very hungry, so Foot-Foot said to Foot-Foot-Foot:

"ere, I'm n'arf 'ungry, why don't you go and nick a lettuce out of Farmer Brown's garden?' (S2)

'You must be joking, Foot-Foot,' said Foot-Foot-Foot. 'I'm the eldest, why don't you go?' (S3)

So Foot-Foot said to Foot: 'Listen Foot, you're the youngest, we're starvin', nip into Farmer Brown's garden and nick us a lettuce.' (S4)

'OK' says Foot. (S5)

So very quickly, Foot runs into Farmer Brown's garden, pinches a lettuce and is just about to run back into his own garden, when . . . BANG! (S6)

Farmer Brown is out with his rifle . . . but . . . phew! He just misses Foot who manages to scurry back with the lettuce. (S7)

'Well done Foot' says Foot-Foot. (S8)

'Well done Foot' says Foot-Foot-Foot. (S9)

'It was nothing' says Foot. (S10)

And they all eat the lettuce. (S11)

Two weeks go by and the rabbits are feeling very hungry again, so Foot-Foot says to Foot-Foot-Foot:

"ere, I'm n'arf 'ungry, why don't you nip into Farmer Brown's garden and nick us a lettuce?' (S12)

'You must be joking, Foot-Foot,' says Foot-Foot-Foot. 'I'm the eldest, why don't you go?' (S13)

So Foot-Foot says to Foot: 'Listen Foot, you're the youngest, we're starvin', nip into Farmer Brown's garden and nick us a lettuce.' (S14)

'OK' says Foot. (S15)

So very quickly, Foot runs into Farmer Brown's garden, pinches a lettuce and is just about to run back into his own garden, when . . . BANG! (S16)

Farmer Brown is out with his rifle . . . and . . . this time he's got Foot, who's lying dead on the ground. (S17)

'Oh dear' says Foot-Foot. (S18)

'Oh dear' says Foot-Foot-Foot. (S19)

And they both cry for Foot. (S20)

Two weeks go by and the rabbits are feeling extremely hungry. (S21)

They've lost a lot of weight and are feeling very weak so Foot-Foot says to Foot-Foot-Foot:

"ere I'm n'arf 'ungry, why don't you go and nick a lettuce out of Farmer Brown's garden?' (S22)

'You must be joking, Foot-Foot,' says Foot-Foot-Foot. 'We've already got one foot in the grave!' (S23)

This shaggy rabbit story provides us with an even more marked example of cohesive symmetry than the Irish joke (see Figure 2). Like the Irish joke, this joke too is structured in threes; there are three symmetrical episodes involving three rabbits whose redundant names when repeated at frequent intervals three times over result in a multiple of three 'Foots'. Furthermore, the text presents a problem and attempts to resolve it.

S1 defines the situation: we are given information about the participants and we are told where the story will take place. This information is correlated with the traditional surface formulaic aperture *Once upon a time there was* . . . Then in S2 we find the first inciting moment in which the story gets going. This inciting moment[2] contains the problem – the rabbits' hunger – and as the story continues we learn of the rabbits' plan to solve the problem until in S6 and S7 we find that the situation intensifies as they are almost thwarted in their attempt to steal a lettuce. This paradigm of 'Situation/Problem/ Solution/Negative solution' is then repeated twice over in the two episodes which follow. In fact, S1 to S11 is the structural blueprint for the second episode.

The situation/problem depicted in S2 is repeated with a variant *two weeks later* in S12. After this we find that the first and second episodes mirror each other perfectly as the dialogues between the rabbits are repeated almost identically; S3 is reflected in S13, S4 in S14 and S5 in S15. However, although S6 mirrors S16, S7 is only partially copied by S17 because the farmer manages to kill Foot and consequently the previous chorus of joy (S8 and S9) becomes a funeral dirge in S18 and S19 when the trio is reduced to a duet:

'Well done Foot' says Foot-Foot. 'Oh dear' says Foot-Foot.
'Well done Foot' says Foot-Foot- 'Oh dear' says Foot-Foot-
   Foot.   Foot.
'It was nothing' says Foot.

The plot reveals an added tangle with Foot's unexpected death and thus comes to a climax. As in any well-respected plot, everything has come to a head. The recipient knows that some sort of confrontation will be inevitable. The initial problem has been resolved but at Foot's expense.

When the plot embarks on the third episode, the symmetry begins in S21 with a reminder of the situation which has now worsened. The recipient is informed about the rabbits' health and expects something to happen which will resolve the situation and take it either to a happy ending or, at least, to a way out. Suddenly, in reply to Foot-Foot's suggestion (S22) we get to the final moment of suspense, as the symmetrical pattern is broken with a punchline (S23). The problem is not resolved but the story concludes with a decent (inde-cent!) ending.[3] Once again we have an expected solution replaced by a pun. As in the Irish joke, nothing explicitly happens and the recipient is left to unravel the pun.

Looking at the breakdown of the joke (Figure 2), we can see how it is that the recipient expects something important to happen to the storyline in the third episode. It is here that the plot deviates most from the norm lain down by the matrix given in the initial episode. Although, of course, the perfect mirroring had begun in the first part of S17, *Farmer Brown is out with his rifle* . . . the utterances which follow in the second episode still match those of the first:

    S7 He just misses Foot →→→→ S17 he's got Foot
S8/9 'Well done Foot' says Foot-Foot →→
                  →→ S18/19 'Oh dear' says Foot-Foot
  'Well done Foot' says Foot-Foot-Foot →→
                →→   'Oh dear' says Foot-Foot-Foot
S11 And they all eat the lettuce →→
            →→ S20 And they both cry for Foot

When we are reminded of the rabbits' hunger in the third episode it is in a more elaborate way than in the previous episodes. We are informed of the details of their weight loss and general health. The narration is expanded for a while only to be contracted again, this time to a synthetic extreme in the punchline.

Fi

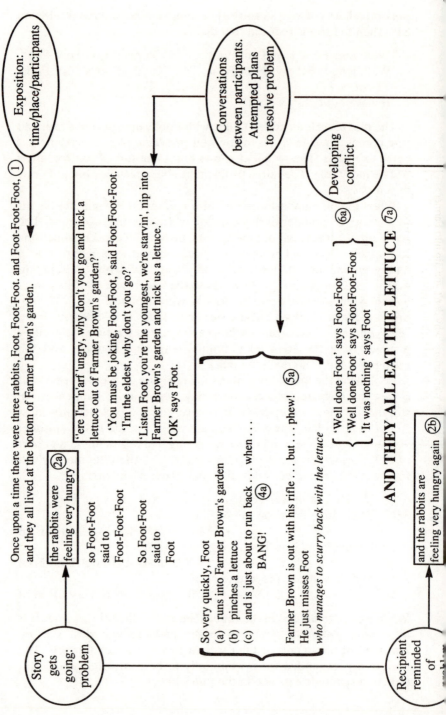

Exposition: time/place/participants ①

Once upon a time there were three rabbits, Foot, Foot-Foot, and Foot-Foot-Foot, ① and they all lived at the bottom of Farmer Brown's garden.

Story gets going: problem

the rabbits were feeling very hungry ②a

so Foot-Foot said to Foot-Foot-Foot

So Foot-Foot said to Foot

Conversations between participants. Attempted plans to resolve problem

'ere I'm 'n'arf 'ungry, why don't you go and nick a lettuce out of Farmer Brown's garden?'

'You must be joking, Foot-Foot,' said Foot-Foot-Foot. 'I'm the eldest, why don't you go?'

'Listen Foot, you're the youngest, we're starvin', nip into Farmer Brown's garden and nick us a lettuce.'

'OK' says Foot.

So very quickly, Foot ④a
(a) runs into Farmer Brown's garden
(b) pinches a lettuce
(c) and is just about to run back ... when ...
BANG! ⑤a

Farmer Brown is out with his rifle ... but ... phew!
He just misses Foot
who manages to scurry back with the lettuce

Developing conflict ⑥a ⑦a

'Well done Foot' says Foot-Foot
'Well done Foot' says Foot-Foot-Foot
'It was nothing' says Foot

AND THEY ALL EAT THE LETTUCE

Recipient reminded of problem

and the rabbits are feeling very hungry again ②b

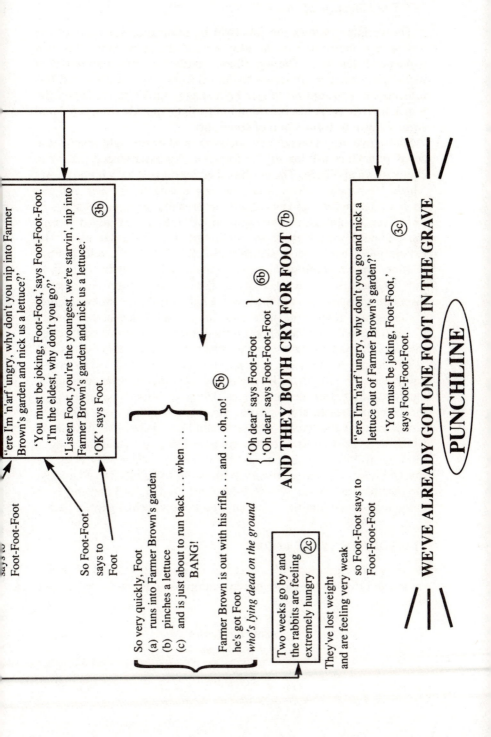

says to
Foot-Foot-Foot

'ere I'm 'n 'arf 'ungry, why don't you nip into Farmer
Brown's garden and nick us a lettuce?'

'You must be joking, Foot-Foot,' says Foot-Foot-Foot.
'I'm the eldest, why don't you go?'

'Listen Foot, you're the youngest, we're starvin', nip into
Farmer Brown's garden and nick us a lettuce.'

'OK' says Foot.

③b

So Foot-Foot
says to
Foot

So very quickly, Foot
(a) runs into Farmer Brown's garden
(b) pinches a lettuce
(c) and is just about to run back . . . when . . . .
BANG!

⑤b

Farmer Brown is out with his rifle . . . and . . . oh, no!
he's got Foot
who's lying dead on the ground

{ 'Oh dear' says Foot-Foot
{ 'Oh dear' says Foot-Foot-Foot } ⑥b

AND THEY BOTH CRY FOR FOOT ⑦b

Two weeks go by and
the rabbits are feeling
extremely hungry ②c

They've lost weight
and are feeling very weak
so Foot-Foot says to
Foot-Foot-Foot

'ere I'm 'n 'arf 'ungry, why don't you go and nick a
lettuce out of Farmer Brown's garden?'

'You must be joking, Foot-Foot,'
says Foot-Foot-Foot.

③c

WE'VE ALREADY GOT ONE FOOT IN THE GRAVE

PUNCHLINE

The recipient knows the joke will be poor and that most of the narrative is inessential to the plot, yet, at the same time, she/he is game and listens to it. The superfluous, redundant information is vital to the performance. It serves to spin the story out; without all this information it would no longer be a shaggy rabbit story. When the punch arrives, what has been spun out will be quickly contracted and shrunk down to form a pun of some sort.

Such a joke relies on performance and, told by the right person, the corny punchline will usually be forgiven. An experienced joker can captivate an audience. The continual crescendo of the rabbits' names which are repeated over and over is pleasing to the ear and the cockney accents will add an extra dimension to the story. Let's face it, Foot-Foot would just not be funny in RP; told in a standard accent, the audience would probably get bored. On the other hand, the expert joker can exploit silences (S6, S7, S16, S17), add gesture (Farmer Brown pointing the rifle, Foot with a hand on his heart as he falls to the ground, etc.) and exaggerated intonation. In a joke, disbelief is suspended, rabbits speak English and plan robberies and, if the person telling the joke can put the audience under a spell through use of accent and good timing, the groan produced through the painfully bad punchline may well be repaid by a sense of catharsis!

The length of the joke is important and is part of the listener's enjoyment. The irrelevancies are interesting, the more information is included, the better the final effect. The joke works intertextually as the listener tries to store all the information given; it is somehow reminiscent of the 'cul-de-sac'-style children's jokes like the one in which we are asked 'If a train is going at 150 m.p.h. and the wind is blowing at 30 m.p.h. in an easterly direction, which way does the smoke blow?' Of course, the train turns out to be electric. Similarly, the listener has no idea where Foot-Foot-Foot, Foot-Foot and Foot are going to lead him/her. Literally, up the proverbial garden path.

THE JOKE IN VERSE FORM

A 'story'-style joke can also occur in verse form. Instead of prose, rhyme and rhythm are exploited to humorous ends when used as joke frames.

> *Alfred de Musset*
> *Hated his pusset*
> *When it mieu'd*
> *He mondieu'd.*

This is a clerihew, a short verse devised around four identical rhymes with a punch in the final couplet. The opening couplet sets the scene by introducing the participant and the situation/problem, while the second and final couplet resolves the problem with a punch. In a way, the clerihew is like a one-liner. Unlike the typical Irish joke in which the narrative is greatly expanded and then quickly contracted into a punch, the clerihew might be compared to the 'condensed' Irish joke (p. 48) as it contracts situation and punch into a single utterance.

Did you hear about the Irishman who bought a zebra and called it Spot?

This clerihew can, in fact, easily be transformed into a one-liner:

Did you hear about the Frenchman who mondieu'd each time his cat mieu'd?

Although both one-liner and clerihew work on the same concept of 'bilingual' punning, which plays as much on the poor English pronunciation of the various 'French' elements as on the invention of portmanteaux, the attraction of rhyme makes the clerihew version a more appealing joke.

Another typical verse frame is the limerick. As Walter Nash puts it:

> Two short stanza types used exclusively for framing jokes are the clerihew and the limerick (possibly the only two wholly British contributions to the art of versification).

> (1985: 52)

Limericks usually follow a rigid scheme regarding rhyme, rhythm and content:

> *There was a young lady of Ryde,*
> *Who ate some green apples and died;*
> *The apples fermented*
> *Inside the lamented,*
> *And made cider inside her inside.*

The two opening lines introduce the protagonist of the limerick and the situation, while the item which occurs at the end of line 2 defines a 'problem' which is expanded upon in the shorter lines 3 and 4 and then finally solved with the punch in the final line. Of course, the place which the protagonist comes from is of vital importance as it determines the rhyme scheme of the whole limerick, since the punch must rhyme with it.

Line 1   There was an old/young woman/man/girl/boy from . . .
(place name) (**RHYME A**)

↓

participant

Line 2   Who had . . . /was/with . . . (**RHYME A**)

↓

situation/problem

Lines 3 & 4   (When) he/she said . . . (**RHYME B**)

↓

expansion of previous situation

Line 5   PUNCH + SOLUTION (**RHYME A**)

Most people would probably agree that Edward Lear's original limericks were not particularly funny, and nowadays most limericks have become obscene:

> *The limerick is furtive and mean,*
> *You must keep her in short quarantine,*
> *Or she sneaks to the slums*
> *And promptly becomes*
> *Disorderly, drunk and obscene.*

However, outside the limerick and the clerihew, poets are inclined to invent their own rhyme schemes.

> *God made things which creep and crawl*
> *But British Rail, it beats them all.*

A quick dig at the punctuality of British Rail in two lines which imply that BR trains move more slowly than snails.

God made things which *creep and crawl* → beetles, spiders, snails, etc.

↓   ↓   ↓

SLOW MOVING

British Rail (*made things*) it beats them all.

↓   ↓

SLOWER THAN

Parodying songs, hymns, advertising jingles and nursery rhymes is a popular children's pursuit.

> *Hey Diddle Diddle,*
> *The Cat and the Fiddle,*
> *The Cow blew up*
> *On the launching pad.*

This version of a children's nursery rhyme defeats the listeners' expectations but remains a puzzle to non-native speakers of English who need to know that in this rhyme the cow is supposed to jump over the moon rather than come to a nasty end.

THE JOKE AS FORMULA

There must surely be as many joke formulae as there are people to tell them, so in this section we will limit ourselves to considering only a couple of the most popular, shorter formulae. Let us begin with formulae in which the senders 'imitate' or rather act out a dialogue point-blank – that is *not* within the frame of a longer narrative structure.

'Mummy, Mummy, can I play with Grandma?'
'No dear, you've dug her up twice this week already!'

'Waiter, waiter, there's a fly in my soup!'
'Don't worry sir, there'll be no extra charge!'

he sender does not embed the exchange within a longer stretch of text, neither does he contextualize it in any way. The dialogue is simply recited out of the blue with the assumption that the recipient will recognize the opening appeals to *Mummy* or *Waiter* as being joke signals. These joke types may well stem from the old music hall formula acted out between comic and stooge which went something like:

'I say, I say, I say, my dog has no nose!'
'Really! Then how does it smell?'
'Awful!'

The opening frame *I say, I say* . . . is simply substituted with *Mummy, Mummy* or *Waiter, waiter*, to signal that a joke is on its way. What is more, the modern exchange is recited by a single speaker who takes on the part of both comic and stooge.

However, dozens of joke types, particularly written graffiti, are structured in terms of a single sentence or utterance. This normally acts as a matrix and serves as the blueprint from which other jokes are generated. For example, from the idiom (of unknown origin) *Old soldiers never die, they just fade away*, we can recognize the following jokes as being its daughters:

Old lawyers never die. They just lose their appeal.

Old DIY enthusiasts never die. They just get plastered.

Old TV directors never die. They just fade to black and white.

Old hippies never die. They just take a trip.

Now, the *old* + *profession/never die/they just* + *pun* formula has generated from a pre-existing idiom, but it is sometimes the case that the reverse occurs and that a joke form injects a new idiom into the language. This is so in the case of 'Smirnoff' jokes. In the mid-1970s the Smirnoff vodka company began using the 'before and after' technique to sell its product. The advertising campaign consisted of escapist photographs accompanied by slogans such as *I thought the Kama Sutra was an Indian restaurant until I discovered Smirnoff*. (The slogan originally had the additional rejoinder *The effect is shattering* which was eventually banned probably due to the allusion to 'getting smashed'.) The slogan turned out to be the inspiration of the graffitists of the nation as catchphrases such as the following began appearing on walls around the country:

I thought innuendo was an Italian suppository until I discovered Smirnoff.

I thought cirrhosis was a type of cloud until I discovered Smirnoff.

However it was not long before the graffitists began to abandon the formula, first by substituting the word Smirnoff with other items:

I thought Nausea was a novel by Jean-Paul Sartre until I discovered Scrumpy.

Soon, the caption began to move more radically away from the matrix, as more items were changed. In the next example there is no allusion to drink whatsoever:

I used to think I was an atheist until I discovered I was God.

Although Smirnoff jokes are now practically obsolete, the *I thought A was B until I discovered C* formula has now frozen into the English language as a semi-idiom. Today we can find graffiti (or indeed hear asides) such as:

I used to talk in clichés but now I avoid them like the plague

in which the original matrix is barely recognizable.

The 'OK' formula

Some formulae, for no apparent reason, suddenly become extremely popular and are not only consequently quoted and heard everywhere, but also manage to survive for several years. The 'OK' graffiti previously mentioned (p. 47) are a good example of how a slogan, inthis case originating from football culture, can be twisted and turned in order to accommodate a joke form.

Anagrams rule – or Luke?

Synonyms govern, all right.

Roget's Thesaurus dominates, regulates, rules, OK, all right, adequately.

Examples rule, e.g.

Dyslexia rules, KO.

Rooner Spules, KO.

Stemming from the matrix *Chelsea rules OK* (where of course 'Chelsea' can be substituted with the football team of one's choice), jokes are generated which set out to parody the original form. The examples above are all to do with the world of language and metalanguage, so in order to 'get' them the recipient must be *au fait* with certain linguistic conventions such as synonymy, the way in which a thesaurus is used, etc.

In order to get these jokes, their recipient must (a) recognize that they are the parody of the 'OK' matrix; (b) possess a certain amount of knowledge regarding dyslexia, Spoonerisms, anagrams, etc.; and (c) recognize that the language itself is being played with.

What it takes to get an 'OK' joke

Knowledge of the matrix

Recognition of subject matter played upon

Linguistic ambiguities of English

RECOGNITION OF JOKE

Anyone who possesses all these prerequisites is also capable of generating his own 'OK' joke. If we want to invent another example of the same formula we know that we must somehow accommodate the matrix to whatever element we have chosen to play upon. Let us remain within the field of language and use the famous linguist Chomsky as the subject for a new example.

We can begin by considering the first half of our joke, which has to be

'Chomsky rules . . .'; after which we must ask ourselves what it is that Chomsky might 'rule' which can be compressed into two upper-case letters; Chomsky's name is linked with language acquisition, universal grammar and transformational-generative grammar, so it won't be long before we come up with:

Chomsky rules, TG.

At this point I may well be accused of having chosen a convenient example; after all, how many other linguists can be so easily linked to an abbreviation. In reply, all I can say is that all jokes work on opportunity, and surely part of the inventor's skill is to seek out the unseen traps of the language and then exploit them for humorous means. Let us try and see if the sphere of language contains any other material for graffiti of this genre:

Tree diagrams rule, NP.

Clarification rules, i.e.

Rather like the 'Smirnoff' construction, the 'OK' formula has almost become an unthinking part of the English language. For example, at the 'Solidarity with Solidarnosc' demonstration in Hyde Park, London on 20 December 1981, a banner was seen which read 'Solidarity ruled OK', while a 'War on Want' advertising campaign of the mid-1980s adopted a brick wall with the graffito: 'Poverty rules OK?'

The 'doing it' formula

A form of word play probably imported to Britain from the United States consists of catchphrases which mildly allude to sex. As we have already discussed, western society finds sex amusing and so consequently it often becomes the subject of jokes and word play. The catchphrases in question, which often appear on car stickers and T-shirts, play on the euphemism of *doing it*, in which *do* is a pro-form clearly standing in for an activity when combined with the pronoun *it*. Undoubtedly, in English, such a combination refers to the sexual act. The typical car sticker will read:

WINDSURFERS DO IT STANDING UP

Unlike the traditional dirty joke, such catchphrases are never sexist and consequently unlikely to offend. However they are rigidly formulaic and must adhere to the following pattern:

SUBJECT +	VERB +	OBJECT +	ADJUNCT
↓	↓	↓	↓
(professional category)	(do)	(it)	(adverb *or* preposition + noun phrase)
TEACHERS	DO	IT	WITH CLASS
ACCOUNTANTS	DO	IT	CALCULATINGLY
CLOWNS	DO	IT	FOR A LAUGH
LINGUISTS	DO	IT	WITH THEIR TONGUES

As we can see, the adjunct can either take the form of an adverb or of a prepositional phrase. Whichever the chosen variable, the punch, realized through the adjunct, must contain a widely shared association with the profession named in the subject. However, variants of the catchphrase exist in which the subject is no longer a professional category but some other social group or even an individual:

PARENTS USED TO DO IT

OSCAR DID IT WILDLY

EINSTEIN DID IT RELATIVELY

As with the 'OK' graffiti, here too it is not difficult to invent our own jokes. How, may we ask, did Mrs Thatcher do it? Conservatively? With an iron fist? With Dennis? There are sure to be those who probably think she doesn't do it at all. And Gorbachev? He must surely do it transparently.

THE JOKE AS ASIDE

The one-liner is an extremely slippery category to classify because so many examples are indeed 'original' in structure and thus impossible to group together with others. What is more, being literally 'one-liners', they are often casually embedded within a conversation and consequently harder to pin down. Unfortunately, many one-liner joke types have been omitted by nature of their very elusiveness; nevertheless, what follows is a rough attempt at categorizing those asides which have allowed themselves to be captured.

Definitions

These are one-liners which normally consist of either an affirmative or an interrogative sentence containing the verb 'to be', in which the definition contains a pun.

An X is someone who . . . = punch + pun

A vegetarian is someone who gives peas a chance.

A romeo is someone who ends all his sentences with a proposition.

When definitions are formed in the interrogative they are posed as naïve rhetorical questions:

Is a red-light district an erogenous zone?

Are eskimos God's frozen people?

Sometimes the pun/punch may occur in the subject:

Is a polygon another name for a dead parrot?

pun = polly (parrot) + gone (dead)

Another variation in form is a noun phrase followed by a dash and another noun phrase which defines the first:

Richard Coeur de Lion – first heart transplant?

However, it is not always the case that such definitions include a pun – they can take the form of cynical comments which are funny to the extent to which they ring true:

The chance of bread falling with the buttered side down is directly pro-portional to the cost of the carpet.

Beauty's only skin deep, but ugly is ugly to the bone.

Exhortations

These jokes are usually found in the form of graffiti which typically consist of an imperative inviting the recipient to do something. The exhortation may include a rejoinder containing a pun.

imperative	*rejoinder + optional pun*
Join the hernia society.	*It needs your support.*
Blow your mind –	*smoke dynamite.*
Save water –	*bath with a friend.*
Help stamp out philately.	

A variant of the above is of course the negative imperative in which the reader is invited *not* to do something. The popular 'down with . . .' graffito can be considered a subcategory of this group of jokes.

Don't let them cut hire education.

Don't vote, the government will get in.

Don't complain about the beer. You'll be old and weak yourself one day.

Down with gravity!

Comments and complaints

These graffiti are more moderate in tone compared with the previous group.

The first group is couched in the third person and posed obliquely, thus giving the impression of not being aimed at anyone in particular. Such comments simply grudgingly declare:

It's not the work that gets me down – it's the coffee breaks.

An apple a day keeps the doctor away but an onion a day keeps everyone away.

A variant of the comment/complaint graffito consists of a name of a famous character followed by a verb and sometimes a noun phrase as well. This time the writer obliquely accuses:

Pablo Picasso paints by numbers.

Andy Warhol stencils.

Cinderella married for money.

Shakespeare eats Bacon. (traditionally followed by the rejoinder: It can't be Donne.)

THE JOKE AS RITUAL

As we have seen, jokes are identifiable by the frame around which they are constructed. Some are built upon the long and complex framework of narrative in which, in order to accommodate a punchline which in itself is a kind of compression of multiple signals and meanings, the text preceding the punch is elaborately expanded. In other cases, a joke can be embedded into a verse form, built around a pseudo-exchange or else generated from the blueprint of a popular catchphrase. In all these cases, the recipient of these funny stories is not expected to interact but simply to listen and finally, it is hoped, to laugh.

However, some jokes do not only depend on the narrator but also require more active participation on the part of the recipient. Instead of just listening, the recipient may actually have to collaborate with the initiator and say something. Interactive jokes range from those which are highly ritualistic in nature, like the 'knock knock' joke, to those made up of a simple question and answer exchange. The archetype of the ritualistic joke must surely be the riddle.

Riddles

A riddle is a brief question and answer exchange between two people, but unlike most question and answer routines the riddle is always answered by the person who posed it in the first place. Nevertheless, this does not mean that the recipient cannot participate actively. At the very least, in answer to the question she must shake her head or say she does not know as a signal to the sender that she is willing to hear the answer.

It is worth remembering that the riddle did not start out as a comic form at all, but rather as a word game in the literal sense of the term. The question posed by the riddle would originally be formulated in rhyme:

> Little Nancy Etticoat
> In a white petticoat,
>   And a red nose,
> The longer she stands
> The shorter she grows.
>   *(1650)*

This deliberately elaborate code represents quite simply a candle. A riddle can, in fact, be defined in terms of a cryptic description of an ordinary object. Nowadays riddles are no longer delivered in rhyme but the cryptic questions still remain. Let us consider the children's classic:

Q.   *What's the difference between a jeweller and a jailor?*

The formula *What's the difference between an X and a Y* is frequently exploited in riddles. Of course, there are dozens of differences between jewellers and jailors; in fact, they are two very odd choices of items to be put up for comparison in the first place. The combination of the *What's the difference . . .* format/opening plus an odd choice of items put up for comparison tells us that we are dealing with humorous discourse. Had the question been something like *What's the difference between a camel and a dromedary?* then it could well have been taken seriously and at face value. However, the absurdity of the question in this particular frame is an indicator of word play. If the recipient is game she will answer that she does not know what the difference is, and, in fact, there is no way she *can* know unless she has heard the riddle before. The answer is: *One sells watches and the other watches cells.* Needless to say, the conundrum is solvable by finding a common denominator which either unites or divides the two items being compared. Once a quality is found which is suitable to one of the items presented in the question, it is then deconstructed in some way to produce a term which can represent a quality inherent in the other item in the riddle. What is interesting about riddles is that their recipients automatically know what their role in the exchange is going to be as soon as they hear the question.

Riddles come in a number of structural variants:

Why is (an) X like (a) Y?

Why did the Z . . .?

When is a K not a K?

What did the big J say to the little J?

Q. *Why is the Tory party known as the cream of society?*
A. *Because it's rich and thick and full of clots.*

Q. *Why did the viper wip'er nose?*
A. *Because the adder 'ad 'er 'andkerchief.*

Q. *When is a door not a door?*
A. *When it is a jar.*

Q. *What did the big chimney say to the little chimney?*
A. *You're too young to smoke.*

Independently of what linguistic options the punch may play on, it will characteristically occur in the answer to the riddle. The half containing the question merely acts as a signal to the recipient that the question is to be taken as an invitation to 'play' and, at the same time, contextualizes the punch itself:

Why did the window box?

The recipient knows a riddle is coming. If he is a native speaker he should also recognize the 'genre' to which it belongs. In a certain sense, the question itself contains a semi-punch because of the way in which the stress deliberately falls 'wrongly' on the 'verb' *box* which for the purposes of the riddle has been extrapolated from a compound noun.

signal that riddle is coming

Q. WHY DID THE WINDOW BOX? → → → *linguistic ambiguity*

A. BECAUSE IT SAW THE GARDEN FENCE.

↓
↓
punch

There are riddles in which the question itself, rather than the answer, more obviously contains the punch:

Q. *What's brown and comes steaming out of cows backwards?*
A. *The Isle of Wight ferry.*

Of course the riddle is meant to be told rather than read, so that the recipient is led to think of a ruminant and not a port. The answer in this example, rather than resolve the conundrum at once, points straight back to the question. The recipient has to then elaborate the homophone /kaʊs/ and the items 'steaming' and 'brown' in the light of a ferry:

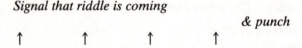

Signal that riddle is coming

& punch

↑   ↑   ↑   ↑

Q. *What's brown and comes steaming out of COWS backwards?*
A. *The Isle of Wight ferry.*

'Knock knock' jokes

The recipient of a 'knock knock' joke has a more active part to play than the recipient of a riddle. The whole ritual is longer and more complex; the joke adheres, in fact, to a rigid five-move exchange between the two participants. Each person knows exactly what to say and when. The recipient's part is indispensable as his role is that of a stooge. The sender of the joke creates a sort of linguistic trap for the recipient to walk into, thus setting up the context for a punch.

Such jokes open with the initiator saying:

1 'Knock, knock!'

The recipient recognizes this as being the initiation of a form of play, therefore, if he or she is game, the obligatory response is:

2 'Who's there?'

As in all opening rituals, the new information is given in the third move:

3 'Mary.'

The rules of the 'game' next oblige the recipient to repeat the name with the addition of the word *who*:

4 'Mary who?'

The punch occurs in the fifth and final move:

5 'Mary Christmas!'

THE JOKE AS REJOINDER

Jokes can even interact with each other. This is the case with the graffito which comments on a graffito which appears above it, which may in turn comment upon one which appears above *it*. It is not at all uncommon to find long, almost never-ending columns of graffiti in different handwriting which all stem from a single graffito.

Home rule for Wales!

This exhortation containing the homophone /ʊeilz/ has prompted another graffitist to scrawl below it:

and Moby Dick for King!

However, rejoinders are not always prompted by a wish to pun. Many, while witty, are simply comments, usually about sex or politics:

When the revolution comes we'll all drive Rolls Royces.

– what if we don't want to drive Rolls Royces?

– when the revolution comes you won't have any choice.

The presupposition contained in the first graffito is the concept of equality which would follow a revolution. The second graffitist misses the point of the egalitarian revolution but plays on the all-inclusiveness of the item *all*, while the final writer puts his finger on the reality of revolutions and comments on the lack of freedom which they inevitably bring about.

Many rejoinders stem from famous quotations:

To do is to be – Rousseau

To be is to do – Sartre

The graffitist who decided to show off her knowledge by quoting Rousseau was quickly followed by another graffitist who quotes Sartre. Both comments are strikingly similar as they contain the same words but arranged differently. A third graffitist was able to follow both quotations with a more down-to-earth, yet equally apt rejoinder – apt in phonological and lexical terms not only because of the play on *do* and *be*, but also because of the handy assonance of *Sartre/ Sinatra*:

Do be do be do – Sinatra

While the written replication is rather limited, since it must adhere quite strictly to the first graffito, the spoken rejoinder can actually expand away from the 'matrix' and keep just a shadow of the original as the text moves on. The Two Ronnies, Ronnie Barker and Ronnie Corbett, frequently used this formula in the pseudo-news broadcasts of their comedy shows.

(. . . and then we'll talk to the man who crossed . . .)

RC: *A skunk with a koala – and got a poo bear.*

RB: *Then he crossed a truss with a polo mint and got a Nutcracker suite.*

RC: *– And a morse code transmitter with a sennapod and got dot dot dot and a very quick dash.*

RB: *He even crossed a food mixer with a nymphomaniac with a lisp – and got a girl who'll whisk anything.*

RC: *And a feather with a lady contortionist and got a girl who could tickle her own fancy.*

RB: *And he actually crossed a table tennis ball with an extremely tall chamber pot and got a ping pong piddle-high poe.*

RC: *Then we talk to a man who crossed a Gordon Highlander with a mousetrap and got a squeaky jockstrap.*

RB: *And to a scientist from Kuwait who's bred an ostrich with a cockscrew head. You give it a fright and it drills for oil.*

The leitmotif of the sequence is the idea of creating silly hybrids from two unlikely objects. The text is made up of eight jokes and each joke works on the principle of the riddle. In order to create the hybrid product of two objects, its author has to find a common denominator of both:

A skunk with a koala – and got a poo bear.

Q.   What happens if you cross a skunk with a koala?
A.   You get a poo bear.

A skunk is an animal which gives out a powerful stench; a koala is a bear and so is Winnie the Pooh; and the word *poo* expresses a bad smell. We have all the necessary elements for a joke.

However, each joke which follows replicates the idea of the hybrid and at the same time tries to better the joke which went before it by inventing a hybrid which is more unlikely than the one which precedes it. The total effect of the text is that of a crescendo of silliness based on a single motif. As the text is performed by two people the final result is not unlike that of a rap.

TWISTING THE FORMULA

Most jokes are predictable, not in the sense that the recipients already know or can easily guess the punch, but because they automatically know that they are about to hear a joke. The recipient knows exactly what to expect apart from the punch itself. However, sometimes these expectations can be foiled if the joker decides to play with the convention itself:

There was an Englishman and an Irishman and . . . BANG!

This joke can be considered qualitatively 'better' than the predictable Irish joke because of this extra element of surprise which it displays. It is doubly clever (or funny) because, as well as the punch, it seems to make fun of itself too.

Often riddles play on the convention of the riddle itself. The classic *Why did the chicken cross the road?* is a perfect example of playground guile, in which the sender of the riddle is tricking the recipient into thinking that they are in the realms of humorous discourse, whereas, in fact, they are not.

Sender: What's the difference between an elephant and a letter box?
Recipient (thinks: Two improbable items are put up for comparison and one
    of them happens to be an elephant . . . this is a riddle.)
    I don't know, what is the difference between an elephant and a letter box?
Sender: I shan't ask you to post a letter then!

The recipient is fooled into thinking that this is a riddle, having been led astray by the opening format and by the content (an elephant being compared to a letter box) of what had seemed to be a riddle. However, the sender wants the question to be taken at face value, as a genuine request for information. The recipient should have answered something like: *An elephant is a huge mammal with a long trunk and ivory tusks, and a letter box is a slit in the door for the delivery of letters.*

There is, of course, no way that the recipient can know whether his interlocutor is being serious or not. As far as he is concerned, he has received all the signals telling him that he is going to be told a joke and that he is in the field of humorous discourse. Then he suddenly finds that he is not.

In the 'knock knock' joke in which *Mary* is turned into *Mary Christmas*, the recipient knows from the start that the initiator will manipulate the word *Mary* in the final move. However, better 'knock knock' jokes break away from the set formula and trick the recipient twice:

'Knock knock!'
'Who's there?'
'The Avon Lady. Your bell's broken.'

The recipient's expectations are defeated as she falls into a pragmatic trap. The normal five-move ritual has been cut short, yet, due to the opening which is recognized as belonging to the original matrix, the recipient is easily deceived into thinking that the initiator wants them to play. Similarly, one child will challenge another with:

'Will you remember me in one day's time?'

The answer will, of course, be 'yes', but then the initiator continues:

'Will you remember me in two day's time?'
('Yes . . .')

'Will you remember me in a week's time?'
('Yes . . .')

The initiator continues increasing the time span until the recipient suddenly hears '*knock knock*', the only response to which can be to ask '*Who's there?*', only to be told: '*There you are, you've forgotten already!*'

As we have seen in the previous chapter, the point at which serious discourse ends and humorous discourse begins is not necessarily well defined. The combination of axial ambiguity together with the manipulation of discourse markers can mislead our interlocutors into thinking we are about to joke when we aren't and vice versa. However, what is happening at a macroscopic level is that the sender is breaking one or more of Grice's co-operative principles. Amongst his maxims of manner we find 'Avoid ambiguity'. All jokes are ambiguous *per se*, so, in a certain sense, every time we tell a joke we are being uncooperative with our interlocutor. If then we joke within the convention of the joke we are surely being doubly ambiguous.

Constantinople is a very long word, can you spell it?

The recipient has no chance of giving the correct answer. If she answers *Constantinople* she will be told that she *can't spell 'it'*. On the other hand, if the recipient sees the trick and spells the pronoun, the sender will then decide that it was the spelling of the city which was required instead. Of course, if I really want you to spell CONSTANTINOPLE and not IT, I make sure that my intonation is such that inverted commas are clearly heard around the IT. This will also stop me from breaking the 'Avoid obscurity of expression' maxim. What is more, such an example is also breaking a maxim of quantity by not being quite as informative as might perhaps have been required. Jokes wantonly throw Grice's maxims to the wind by their very nature, but usually the recipient will know what is coming from the frame. *Have you heard the one about . . .? Why is an X like a Y?* – these openings give the listener some warning to momentarily suspend disbelief. As we have seen, some examples are doubly cruel/clever because they arrive without warning – or rather, they give a 'false' warning. In the example just quoted we are faced with a normal question frame. There are no Irishmen, no elephants and no odd comparisons. Not unreasonably, the recipient tries to test his knowledge of spelling, yet soon finds that no spelling is the right spelling.

Playing with or twisting the pragmatic or social rules of language so as to confuse our interlocutors into not knowing whether we are being serious or asking them to 'play' could well be labelled verbal 'guile'. This could be considered a verbal stratagem, the aim of which is to trap the recipient into saying something wrong so that the laugh will be at his expense. In fact, such forms of word play are particularly popular amongst schoolchildren, who from a very early age realize that getting one up on their chums makes them (a) feel good and (b) look clever in front of their peers.

Children's verbal tricks cover every possible linguistic option imaginable.

If frozen water is iced water, what's frozen ink?

Do you learn Guzzinta at your school?

No doubt we all recall the embarrassment of saying something stupid, of falling into a trap while our interlocutor gains points.

The openings of children's catch questions are innocent sounding:

You know your great-great-great-great-great grandmother?

In no way does this question contain a joke frame so the recipient is bound to interpret *you know* as the pragmatic marker it normally is in conversation, i.e. 'I'm drawing attention to something I'm about to say.' The retort:

Ha, ha, ha, no you don't because she's dead!

plays on the face value of the items *you* and *know* and not on their functions as text markers. The joke is not introduced within its normal or expected frame. A question and answer style joke is presented as a direct challenge; it will contain signals informing the recipient that she will hear a conundrum and it will probably also be defined by an absurd question like:

What's green, with four brown legs, twenty-two balls and if it fell on top of you out of a tree would kill you?

It would be clearly out of the question to expect anyone to know that the answer is:

A snooker table.

On the contrary, if a child is told:

I know what you're going to say next . . .

she may well answer 'What?' because of the lack of any signal indicating that the remark does not belong within the realms of serious discourse. Naturally, she will then be told: 'I knew you'd say "what".'

NOTES

1 There appears to be no technical term for the punchline; however it has been previously labelled both *paesis* (Hockett, 1977) and *locus* (Nash, 1985).

2 Labels regarding surface and notional structure are those of Longacre (1983: 22).

3 Longacre (1983: 21) writes, 'Conclusion, 'Wrap it up', brings the story to some sort of decent – or indecent – end.'

4   Translating word play

Anyone who has ever tried to translate an English joke into another language will know that it is no easy task. No matter how well the translator knows the target language, cultural references and polysemous items may well involve them in longwinded explanations, after which the recipient rarely reacts with a laugh. Similarly, when a joke in a foreign language is translated into English, results tend to be equally disastrous. Jokes, it would seem, travel badly.

In the opening chapter we considered what, if anything, was funny intra-culturally. Slapstick, for example, was seen to be funny in all western cultures, and transcultural problems reared their heads only when language became involved. Nevertheless, to suggest that a common linguistic code is all that is needed in order to appreciate jokes and word play would be extremely naïve. One only has to consider the numerous American situation comedies which have had little or no success in Britain, and vice versa, to see that a shared code is only half the story. Language and culture seem to be indivisible and, without shared sociocultural knowledge between sender and recipient, a common linguistic code will be of little help.

Edward Sapir and Benjamin Lee Whorf claimed that each language together with its individual sounds, words and syntax, reflects a separate social reality which is different from that which is reflected in another. Consequently, translation is not simply a matter of substituting the words of one language with those of another and adapting the syntax to suit it. For a translation to be successful, the translator has also to convey a whole store of added meaning belonging to the culture of the original language.

> No two languages are ever sufficiently similar to be considered as representing the same social reality. The worlds in which different societies live are distinct worlds, not merely the same world with different labels attached.
>
> (Whorf 1956, 69)

The intertwining of formal linguistic features and sociocultural elements contained in a joke is often so specific to a single language community that, beyond its frontiers, the joke is unlikely to succeed. This is why speakers of British English do not necessarily 'get' jokes told in American or Australian English and vice versa.

SHARED CODE AND SHARED CONVENTIONS

If two cultures possess categories of jokes which play on similar subject matters – in other words, if parts of both worlds somehow match – then it ought to follow that translating jokes into the two reciprocal languages should be a fairly easy task.

Let us begin by examining 'underdog' jokes. Most cultures have a tradition of jokes which poke fun at a minority group of some sort. In many French jokes, Belgians are depicted as witless underdogs; in the United States, the imbeciles are the Poles; and their place is taken by the Portuguese in Brazil and the Irish in England. Consequently, any 'underdog' joke should be able to be translated quite easily by simply replacing the underdog of the original joke with the underdog of one's choice.

1
Recently heard over the loudspeakers at Heathrow airport:
Air France – Flight 106, departing 2.30 p.m., Gate 12
British Airways – Flight 22, departing 2.35 p.m., Gate 10
Polish Air – Flight 157, when the little hand is on the four and the big hand is on the twelve, Gate 5.

It would be quite sufficient to substitute Polish Air with Aer Lingus to obtain the English version of this American joke. However, minority groups do not necessarily have to be of the ethnic variety. In Italian society, for example, England's thick Irishman is replaced by a *carabiniere*, a member of one of Italy's three police forces.

2
Did you hear the one about the Irishman/carabiniere who went water-skiing and then spent the whole holiday looking for a sloping lake?

3
Perché i carabinieri lavorano sempre in coppia?
Perché ci vuole uno per leggere ed uno per scrivere.

(Why do carabinieri/Irishmen always work in twos?
So that one can read and one can write.)

Even when the minority group is not of the ethnic variety, the underdog can still be replaced by the underdog normally found in similar jokes told in the target language. It is almost as though the underlying message of these jokes is identical; what varies is simply the surface elements. Thus it would seem that it is simply a question of being *au fait* with the cultural joking mores of each language community to translate efficiently.

However the worlds of two cultures do not always match quite so easily. When dealing with another joke 'universal', sex, there are rather more complex difficulties to be faced when attempting to translate. Despite the fact that most western cultures see sex as humorous subject matter, they do so in slightly different ways.

Within the category of the dirty joke there are dozens of variations and they do not necessarily match transculturally. Many dirty jokes do indeed have in common features such as female degradation and male sexual prowess, which are identical despite geographical boundaries, yet this universal double standard becomes multi-faceted according to each individual culture.

4
Due bambini litigano:
– Mio padre è migliore del tuo!
– Non è vero!
– Mio fratello è migliore del tuo!
– Non è vero!
– Mia madre è più buona della tua!
– Beh . . . questo lo dice anche Papà!

(Two boys are arguing:
– My Dad's better than yours!
– Oh no he's not!
– My brother's better than yours!
– Oh no he's not!
– My mother's better than yours!
– Well . . . I suppose that's true 'cos my Dad says so too!)

Although most English speakers see what the joke is getting at, it does not quite work. First, there are problems regarding the translation of the item *più buona*. In this context, the English version really requires post-modification with *in bed*, but this would have spoilt the effect of the triple re-iteration of *better*. Second, the sexuality of men's mothers is not seen as a form of filial cuckoldry in Britain in the same way as it still is in Italy (see Chapter 1, p. 10).

Thus the joke works on (a) the cleverness of the successful male adulterer (and his complice son) and (b) the one-upmanship of the boy who can now accuse his antagonist of being the son of an adulteress. An English version of the same theme can be seen in the following joke:

5

'Mummy, Mummy, does the au pair girl come apart?'
'No dear, why do you ask?'
'Because Daddy says he's just screwed the arse off her!'

Apart from problems deriving from the translation of *screw* and *come apart* this joke would present no real difficulties in comprehension to the foreign recipient. Here too, as in the Italian joke, a child is responsible for letting out the truth. In British culture the degraded female becomes an au pair girl, who together with the cuckolded wife becomes the object of the joke. Both jokes prize the successful adulterer, yet, while the Italian recipient would recognize the theme of male prowess in the au pair joke, the British recipient of the translated Italian joke is not going to see the joke in its entirety.

Similarly, the force of the French retort *Et ta soeur?* scribbled beneath the graffito *Froggies go home!* is bound to be lost on its recipients. Literally translated *And what about your sister?*, it would mean very little to most people. Although it would probably be best translated with something like *Why don't you go to hell!*, the source version is actually insulting the recipient through his sister by suggesting she is sexually active. As in Italian culture, reference to sisters' and mothers' sexuality can be insulting.

These three examples back up the Sapir–Whorf hypothesis regarding the intertwining of language and social reality. In one culture we find the verbalization of the disapproval, and, above all, the filial shame involved in a mother's illicit sexual behaviour being so strongly ingrained that it can become the basis for a put-down joke, while in another the same concepts are non-existent. The English joke supports the adulterer and the recipient laughs at him simply because he happens to have been found out. In other cultures he can be ridiculed through the sexuality of female members of his family.

DIFFERENT CODES AND ABSENCE OF REFERENCE

As we have seen, when the two languages involved in the translation of a joke possess even a little shared cultural ground with each other, although the target version will not always be perfectly clear to the recipient, it will at least bear some resemblance, content-wise, to the message in the original text. Nevertheless, not all jokes are about an underdog or sex. Many play on events, states and situations which are peculiar to their culture of origin. Naturally such jokes create serious problems, not as far as the technicalities of translation are concerned, especially if no punning is involved, but for the recipient's understanding.

The Chinese cartoon in example 6 is by Gang Zhie Ye.

6

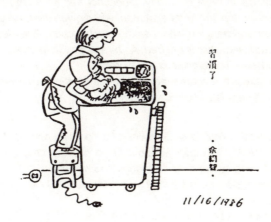

from *The People's Daily*

'Used to it'
After saving money for quite some time, the family has finally bought a washing machine. Days later, the son comes home from school to find his middle-aged mother standing on a small stool and handwashing clothes with a washboard inside the brand new washing machine. Puzzled, the son asks, 'Why don't you use the machine, Mama?' 'I am just used to doing it this way.'

The translation is more than adequate, yet, to a European audience, it can hardly be considered as being funny. The analyst (and translator) of the joke, Yan Zhao, explains that it plays on the influence of old traditions and the confusion caused to the Chinese by modernization. The recipient's amusement lies in the mother's fusion/confusion of new and old, technical and manual (Zhao, 1988).

Of course, not all westerners will be able to read between the lines of the joke and see it in its entirety. In fact, the analyst himself points out that the translation above is, at the same time, an expansion of the original text. While, on the one hand, to the westerner it conveys new information about modern China, it is still not easy to see why it should be funny, without prior knowledge of Chinese attitudes.

Similarly, those of us who are not totally *au fait* with German culture will remain slightly perplexed when trying to come to terms with the nation's political jokes.

7a

Following a scandal in West Germany, Genscher and Kohl are condemned to death. Genscher, the first to be executed, when given the choice between the electric chair and hanging, chooses the electric chair. The electric chair is out of order and Genscher is set free. As he leaves the execution chamber he whispers to Kohl, 'The electric chair is broken!'
Kohl enters the execution chamber and, when given the choice between the electric chair and hanging, chooses hanging.

7b

Following a scandal in Germany, Genscher, La Fontaine and Kohl are facing a firing squad. When Genscher is about to be shot he shouts out 'Earthquake!' and the firing squad drop their guns and run away.
When La Fontaine is about to be shot he shouts out 'A flood!' and the firing squad drop their guns and run away.
When Kohl is about to be shot he shouts out 'Fire!'

Naturally, the non-German will recognize Kohl as the underdog, but a translation in which he is substituted with an Irishman could hardly be considered wholly satisfactory. Both are political jokes which express some Germans' view of their premier. The substitution of Kohl with the British premier would be equally inadequate since, though he may be considered many things, he is not generally considered to be an imbecile. Furthermore, as with the Chinese joke, these jokes too convey to the recipient new information about their country in the 1990s: in this case Germany's embarrassment and fear of political scandals.

Shared knowledge is not only restricted geographically. Shortly after the violent earthquake which took place in southern Italy in the winter of 1980, there was a sudden fashion for earthquake jokes. The one which follows is now just as meaningless in Italian today as it is in English, because the earthquake has now become a distant memory. The joke plays on the scandals which came to light after the earthquake regarding the embezzlement of funds which were supposed to have been used for building materials. Damaged caused by the earthquake itself was heightened due to the quality and quantity of reinforced concrete used in many of the city's buildings.

8

Cosa rispose il cemento armato quando il pilastro gli chiese come si sentiva dopo il terremoto?
– Come sempre, tanto, io non c'ero!

(What did the reinforced concrete say when the iron beam asked him how he felt after the earthquake?
– Fine, after all, I wasn't there!)

Without the explanation given above, the joke would have made little or no sense to most non-Italians; with the explanation, it can hardly be considered a joke. Similarly, the graffito at Orly airport which reads: *De Gaulle est pire qu'Hitler. Mais plus con* (*De Gaulle is worse than Hitler but more foolish*) is now out of date. It was probably witty in the 1960s, but today the only element which could be mildly amusing about the quip is the double meaning of the taboo item *con*.

Thus, the success of translated jokes does not necessarily depend upon the quality of translation. In many cases what may appear to be a poor joke may exclusively depend on gaps in the recipient's world knowledge – or rather in her knowledge of the day-to-day affairs of the 'translated' culture. It is worth bearing in mind that Italian young people, for example, would not have understood the earthquake joke either, owing to the fact that, in the joke, the strength of sociocultural knowledge overrides the importance of linguistic competence.

Naturally, the same problems can occur when translating from English into other languages. If we consider a joke from the 1950s which is equally as meaningless today in Britain as the earthquake and De Gaulle jokes in Italy and France, we will clearly see that we are faced with similar problems.

9

Q.   *If Christie had two sons what would he call them?*

A.   *Ropem 'n Chokem*

Now we can see that trickier problems regarding the translation of jokes begin when linguistic features create a further obstacle to the kind of culture-specific difficulties previously suggested. If we try to produce an Italian version, the punchline becomes *Legale e Strozzale*, two names with feminine endings which are grammatically incompatible with the masculine plural 'subject', Christie's sons. On the other hand, the alternative 'i' ending would be just as incorrect, since Christie's victims, to which the terms refer, were exclusively female. Both solutions therefore create havoc with Italian rules of concord.

A more extreme example can be found in the title of a medieval parody of courtly love, the French fabliau: *Guillaume et le Falcon*.

The hypothetical translation 'William and the Falcon' would only be acceptable on one level. *Falcon* is indeed a falcon, but, in French, *falcon* is pronounced /faʊkɔ/, which, when deconstructed, becomes *faus con* = 'false cunt'. In modern Italian we find:

10
Qual è la storia d'Italia in tre parole?
Dux, Crux, Crax.

(The history of Italy in three words: Dux, Crux, Crax.)

The punchline consists of two Latin words: *dux* = 'leader' and *crux* = cross. As is well known, Mussolini was *Il Duce*, 'The Leader', and the cross is the symbol of the Christian Democrat party which has dominated Italian politics since the Second World War. The item *Crax* is the focal point of the joke; it is a pseudo-Latin word formed from the name *Craxi*, which neatly fits in with the rhyme and rhythm of the preceding two items. Bettino Craxi is the leader of the Socialist party and has played a leading role in recent parliamentary affairs.

The conclusion to be drawn is quite clear: when sociocultural restraints are combined with linguistic restraints, translation can become an arduous task. Roman Jakobson (1959) is more drastic in his claims when he states that full equivalence in translation is impossible. Undoubtedly, although the translations of the jokes considered so far are perfectly adequate, none of them are truly equivalent.

Even the first group of jokes analysed (i.e. the 'underdog' jokes), which had an equivalent category in English culture, involved slightly falsified translations. Although it was possible to substitute one minority group for another, real equivalence is actually lost because Poles and Irishmen and *carabinieri* cannot be substituted for each other if the aim is true equivalence. Conversely, as was seen in examples 4 and 6, when true equivalence remains after translation, a joke can then become a non-joke due to lack of cultural references.

PARTICULAR PROBLEMS INVOLVED IN JOKE TRANSLATION

The linguistic problems inherent in the translation of jokes, and the questions regarding language/society and equivalence considered so far are problems which exist in the interlingual translation of all texts, whether humorous or not. However, jokes and word play do present some extra difficulties not encountered in translating straight referential prose, which, as we shall see, compare with the difficulties faced in the translation of literary texts and especially poetry.

If it were not for the cues given by canned laughter, many jokes and humorous quips occurring in foreign versions of imported American comedies could easily pass by unnoticed. Despite signals which indicate that someone has just said something funny, it is not always the case that the audience is going to be amused by the translated quip. It would appear that translators are often afraid of moving away from the text and replacing an untranslatable joke with another one which would work in the target language, even if it is completely different from the original. They are reminiscent of the famous translation scholar Lévy who believed that the translator had to handle all problems in a text no matter how difficult, while at the same time, respecting both style and form. Consequently, in the Italian version of *The Big Chill*, the puzzled glance which Kevin Kline gives to his jeans when asked to father the leading lady's child because of his good genes is totally lost because the translator has her declare '*Hai dei buoni geni . . .*' ('*You've got good genes*'), where the Italian item *geni* is purely monosemous and bears no phonological resemblance to the word 'jeans' (*geni* = /dgeni/).

Eugene Nida (1964) suggests that the translator analyses the source language text and then restructures it when transferring it to the target language. In other words, the source text should first be decoded and then recoded in such a way that will make perfect sense in the target language.

SOURCE LANGUAGE TEXT	TARGET LANGUAGE TEXT

genes /dginz/ =
unit of hereditary
chromosome
    ↓
(homophone of jeans =
casual trousers)   → → → → → →   jeans /dginz/ =
casual trousers

geni /dgeni/ =
units of hereditary
chromosome

NO EQUIVALENT ITEM
?????????????????

As we can see from this attempt at restructuring the joke into the target language, there is no way of retaining source meaning. Once the translator had realized that the same homophony of the English items *jeans/genes* was non-existent in Italian, her best ploy would probably have been that of abandoning the joke altogether and perhaps substituting it with a completely different Italian one. In exchange for the loss of equivalence she would have gained some sort of functional equivalence by having replaced a joke with another joke. As the text presently stands, the audience is faced with a *non sequitur*.

Of course, it is easy for speakers of more than one language to be hard on translators when their task is indeed near-impossible, yet their fear of substitution is not easily understandable. Even a totally different comment, in place of an untranslatable joke, would often be preferable to translation 'gaffes'. In the film *Space Balls*, when a gigantic jar of jam comes hurtling through the sky, it is clearly seen as a *'space traffic jam'*; *'una marmellata di traffico spaziale'* does not have the same meaning at all in Italian, where a traffic jam is simply an *ingorgo* and nothing to do with conserves of fruit and sugar, *marmellata*. Of course, there are dozens of similar examples which can be found in screen comedies in translation. Many exchanges in the Italian version of Stephen Spielberg's *Who Framed Roger Rabbit* appear quite meaningless, yet suspicions that such *non sequiturs* were merely instances of utterances in which either the translator had not seen the joke or had decided to translate it at face value were proven to be well-founded each time an odd sounding remark was mentally translated back into a more likely sounding original. For example, when Roger Rabbit asks Bob Hoskins what he thinks of show business, and, in the original version of the film, he replies *'There's no business like it'*, we can safely bet that it was intended as a witty remark. Italian has neither a song of that title nor a saying which echoes it, so a one-to-one translation of the remark not only is not funny but has no cultural referent either.

These examples from the cinema present the translator with a dilemma, since in both cases she needs to find a remark which conveys a similar meaning, with the additional problem that it should be witty too. Susan Basnett-McGuire (1980, 22) supplies the translator of a play with the following guidelines:

(1)   Accept the untranslatability of the source language phrase in the target language on the linguistic level.

(2)   Accept the lack of a similar convention in the TL.

(3)   Consider the range of TL phrases available, having regard to

the presentation, status, age, sex of the speaker, his relationship to the listeners and the context of the meaning in the SL.

(4) Consider the significance of the phrase in its particular context – i.e. as a moment of high tension in the dramatic text.

(5) Replace in the TL the invariant code of the SL phrase in its two referential systems (the particular system of the text and the system of the culture out of which the text has sprung).

Let us try to apply these criteria to the translation of *'There's no business like show business.'* Once we have accepted that there can be no linguistic or cultural equivalence, we must begin examining the range of target language phrases available. If we accept the item (and concept of) *business* as the invariant core of the target language phrase, a likely candidate picked from the array of Italian idioms which include the word *business/affari*, could be *Gli affari sono affari* ('Business is business'). While not particularly witty, it is a more natural Italian phrase than an oblique reference to an idiom which does not exist at all.

Jokes which are too culture-specific are not easily understood beyond their country of origin. Although translation is possible, it is not necessarily going to be meaningful. Similarly, jokes which are too 'language-specific' are doomed to suffer the same fate as those in the film examples mentioned above. However, jokes in which sociocultural references cross-cut play on language are the most difficult of all to render in another language. As we saw previously (cf. Charles Hockett, p. 124), some jokes can be seen as being formally similar to literary prose and others as being similar to poetry. One of the most convincing arguments to support such a division is that so-called 'poetic' jokes, those which are 'language-specific', present many of the same problems as poetry when they are translated.

The following joke apparently presents no particular linguistic idiosyncrasies or ambiguities and thus could be compared to a short piece of prose:

11

'Mummy, Mummy, I don't want to go to France!'
'Shut up and keep swimming!'

Such a joke does not rely on language for its punch and would present no particular problems in translation or understanding to a member of any culture which adopts modern means of transport for travelling. On the other hand,

12
Nothing succeeds like a parrot

would be considered as more 'poetic' in nature. It relies on the duplicity and deconstruction of one particular language item for its punch, so, for a perfect translation to be achieved, the target language would need to possess a word for 'succeeds' which, when taken apart, can become both verb and noun which refer to the eating habits of a parrot (or any other seed-sucking animal). As such close linguistic similarity between two languages is highly unlikely, a good translation is difficult to achieve. Like the punster, the poet, too, has at her disposal a variety of options within the language which she can exploit to create a humorous effect. As these options tend to be typical only of the source language, it follows that poetry and puns tend to encounter similar difficulties when an attempt is made at translation. Traditional poetry involves rhyme, rhythm and metre and the visual schemes adopted in more contemporary forms are features which by their very nature cannot find exact equivalents in another language. Therefore, in no way can a perfect mirroring of a poetic form be achieved. Naturally, the translator of a Shakespearean sonnet is likely to have to deal with a greater number of features which are idiosyncratic to the source language than the translator of joke 12 who only has to overcome the problem attached to the item *succeeds*. Yet some jokes are worth comparing to poetry in terms of the density of translation obstacles to be overcome and, whether easy or difficult to translate, like poetry, they are not exactly mirrored in their translated form.

A brief glance at an example of comic verse in Russian is sufficient to demonstrate an extreme example of untranslatability, or rather the numerous compromises which translators must sometimes make:

13   СВЕРХУ МОЛОТ
            СНИЗУ СЕРП
            ЭТО – НАШ
            СОВЕТСКИЙ ГЕРБ
            ХОУЕШБ – ЖНЙ,
            АХОЧЕШБ КУЙ,
            ВСЕ РАВНО
            ПОЛУЧИШБ
            ХУЙ!

Below – the sickle
Above – the hammer:
This is the seal on our Soviet banner.
Whatever in life

you choose to do,
It's all the same:
You still get screwed.

The target version is qualitatively good, yet, by the very nature of the different alphabets and sound systems involved, the result is a different poem.

It is undeniable that poetry exploits the linguistic features inherent in a language, sometimes to the point of exasperation as, for example, in the case of concrete poetry, and consequently translations of jokes which rely heavily on linguistic exploitation, as the example above does, are more of an interpretation than a translation. However, to imply that the opposite is true for prose (and consequently 'prosaic' jokes) is to oversimplify matters. Poetic language cannot be restricted to 'high-flown' poetry alone; in other words, it cannot only be seen in terms of alliteration, paranomasia, dactyl metre and so forth. Such a view is quite the opposite of Jakobson's more elastic interpretation of poetry, which goes as far as including the poetic function within the referential function. According to Jakobson, prose itself is a continuum in which the referential function and the poetic function are intertwined to varying degrees. Seen in such a light, jokes which rely on linguistic manipulation would occur at the poetic extreme of our imaginary continuum.

If literary prose and jokes are closer to the poetic end of this hypothetical cline than 'practical' prose, then the question could be seen in terms of differentiation between playing *with* language and playing *through* language; we could say that, roughly speaking, the former occurs in poetry and the latter in literary prose. In either case a deviance from 'pure' referential prose occurs. Since jokes are indeed examples of creative use of language which, like literature, breaks pre-established patterns of clearly referential prose, then, in Jakobsonian terms, any joke by definition could be seen as being 'poetic', whether linguistically or socioculturally inclined. While some jokes play *with* language, others simply play *through* it.

Let us consider 'OK' jokes (see p. 28), which belong to a graphological convention which does not exist in non-English-speaking countries. Owing to the fact that these jokes acquire their meanings through reference to other examples of the same type of graffiti, speakers of other languages would need to possess prior knowledge of the genre of graffiti in order to understand and appreciate them. Outside the context created by the genre itself, clever as the play may be, it will remain meaningless. Clearly, the parallel with 'real' literature can now be taken a step further as the aspect of intertextuality inherent in these jokes becomes evident. Someone who is well-read is more likely to recognize the multitude of historical and literary references included in Umberto Eco's *The Name of the Rose* than a reader who has read less widely. Such recognition adds to the pleasure of the text and gives a new dimension to what would otherwise have been no more than a detective story. Something similar occurs in a good joke. 'OK' graffiti are clever rather than funny; at a glance the 'expert' recipient recognizes the text type and links it to its previous counterparts and then connects the graffito to his or her world knowledge. The pleasure of such a text is gained through the author's skill in playing with the language plus the reader's ability to extract the inner meaning of the text. Due to the idiosyncratic graphological elements involved, 'OK' jokes only work when they are seen. Their translation is impossible without the loss of their full significance. A translation would require a complex explanation of how they have derived from a slogan and developed into a joke form. After such an explanation the text would cease to function as a joke.

The visual features exploited in each 'OK' joke are specific to English and English alone. As well as having to cope with difficulties inherent in the matrix itself, the translator would have to cope with the unavailability of one-to-one graphological equivalents.

14
Apathy ru

Dyslexia rules KO

Similar difficulties occur when trying to translate examples of humorous/clever graffiti which occur in other languages. It would appear that the 'OK' genre, and in fact joke genres in general, only occur in English-speaking communities, so the difficulty of dealing with graffito type does not seem to apply in other languages.

15
LIBERTÉ – EGALITÉ – FRATERNITÉ
– Maternité!

This graffito appears outside a hospital in Paris and the word *Maternité* is a rejoinder to the first scrawl. A translation into English of the rejoinder would be self-evident and, since the revolutionary slogan is well known in its source form, in the same context in both languages we thus produce a witty remark. Conversely:

16
Je suis Marxiste – tendance Groucho

causes problems as 'I'm a Marxist with Groucho tendencies/leanings/ sympathies' hardly sounds English, although most people could clearly see what the writer is trying to play on. Similarly the Flemish graffito,

17
Kan een professor in de hemel komen?
Ja, want God is oneiiiiidig goed.

(Can a professor get to heaven? Yes, because God is infiniiiiitely good.)

while conveying the unpopularity of university dons, leaves the non-Belgian wondering why the 'i' is lengthened.

The following graffito was scribbled in the proximity of a stall selling strawberries in Naples on the first Mothers' Day after the local football team had won the league cup. It plays on a combination of language (Neapolitan dialect) and a visual cue:

18
P'a mamma e Maradona
accattateve 'o

(Buy some strawberries for your mothers and Maradona.)

The recipient has to add the word *fraulonë* (Neapolitan for 'strawberry'; standard Italian: *fragolone*) to rhyme with Maradona, which in Naples is pronounced with a final /ə/. Furthermore, the non-Neapolitan recipient will need to understand the significance of the term *mother* matched with the name of a famous football star. Maradona has been put on a pedestal on a par with Italian mothers, who are venerated in Italian culture. What the joker is suggesting is that Maradona is as much loved as a mother. The English equation of 'mother + Maradona' has no such connotation.

My poor translation speaks for itself. It has neither the rhyme, the rhythm nor the dynamism of the original and is consequently unpoetic, unfunny and not in the slightest bit clever. Of course, a professional translator could have done the quip more justice by replacing the original with a different rhyme, but in no way could they have kept the integral form and meaning and at the same time given all the necessary information to allow the foreign reader to appreciate it fully.

The question of untranslatability has been brought up by many theorists (e.g. Jakobson, 1959 and Popovic, 1976) and their arguments can be seen very clearly when it comes to jokes like the 'OK', 'Maradona' and Russian examples we have just considered. Clearly any translation is by its very nature an interpretation of the source text rather than its perfect reflection. Translation seems to be a necessary evil, never quite right but indispensable all the same.

While graffiti may seem to present the translator with especially difficult problems, oral jokes are certainly no less exacting. A perfect interlingual translation of the playground classic:

19
What's black and white and red (read) all over?

is, technically speaking, impossible. Unlike the 'OK' graffiti which had to be read, this riddle has to be spoken, since, visually, it cannot work because of the fact that although *red* and *read* are homophones they are not also homographs. In French, Italian and German the items *rouge, rosso, rot* have no meaning other than 'red' and neither do they possess a homophone. The translator, in this case, is forced to sacrifice what Eugene Nida (1964) defines 'formal' equivalence, for 'dynamic' equivalence. In other words, the text is seen as a process, the function of which is to amuse and stimulate laughter. Since, in this case, the text is an attempt at being funny or clever, what the translator can do is to substitute the text with another which serves an identical purpose. However, not any joke will do. If we consider the newspaper as being the invariant core – in other words the piece of information which is vital to the source text and thus has to remain in the target version – we could rely on a metaphorical use of the item *red* to keep the target joke in line with the source joke. In French, we could then come up with:

Qu'est qui/Quel journal est tout rouge et noir et blanc?
L'Umanité.

L'Umanité is the newspaper which represents the French Communist party, and the item *rouge* possesses the same political connotation as it does in English. Unfortunately, however, native French speakers neither see the joke as being funny nor even clever. Such a translation would have to be revised.

Conversely, if we use the same metaphorical use of *red* to produce an Italian translation, the result is more satisfactory:

Quale giornale è rosso, bianco e nero?
L'Unità.

In translation, formal equivalence is lost on several levels. First, as in the French version, the word-order of the colour adjectives changes as Italian prefers the order of *bianco e nero* ('white and black') to the marked *nero e bianco*, and, for similar reasons of prosodic naturalness, *rosso* ('red') must precede them both. Second, the Italian conundrum asks 'Which newspaper is black and white and red?'; whereas the English riddle avoids any allusion to newspapers until the answer (in the French version, mentioning the newspaper is optional). If the Italian version had avoided including the newspaper in the question, presenting it only in the punch, the punch itself would have had no meaning because no item in the question refers to reading, either through homophony, homonymy or any other kind of duplicity. The choice of *L'Unità*, the daily newspaper which is the official organ of the Italian Communist party,[1] conveniently fulfils the need to satisfy the inclusion of Popovic's 'invariant core', since it unites both source and target texts by means of its connotation with both 'read' and 'red'. To a certain degree, dynamic equivalence has been held, although the English riddle is a homophonic pun and the target version plays on a metaphorical use of 'red'.

If we try to produce a German version of this joke, the newspaper must not appear in the question as this would render the conundrum too obvious:

Was ist rot, schwarz und weiss?
Die Tageszeitung.

As in the Italian version, German prefers a different word-order for the colour adjectives. A feasible solution to the choice of newspaper falls on *Die Tageszeitung* which represents independent left-wing politics.

The question of the 'invariant core' seems to be crucial to successful translation. Once this core has been found, the translator's job is simplified. However, convenient 'cores' are not always at hand for the benefit of interlingual translation. *The Children of Dynmouth* by William Trevor provides us with many quips which are extremely tricky to translate.

20
'Well, have a plum' said the doctor in an effeminate voice. 'If you swallow the stone whole you'll put on weight.'

The Italian translators[2] decided that the 'invariant core' necessary to both source and target texts was something inherent in the concept of weight. In Italian, the word 'stone'/*pietra* cannot refer in any way to weight – and even if it could, an Italian plum contains a *nocciolo*/

'kernel' and not a stone. In order to overcome this problem, the Italian doctor offers a thrush instead of a plum.

– *Manga i tordi, egli gli disse in falsetto.*
– *Così ingrasso dottore?*
– *Cinguetti!*

The substitution of 'plum' with *tordi*/'thrushes' gives the translators an opportunity to use the verb *cinguettare*, which means 'to chirp'. A deconstruction of the second person singular of the verb, i.e. 'you chirp', results in /tʃɪnɡʊetɪ/ a homphone of *cinque etti* (an *etto* is a measure of weight which is equivalent to a hundred grams).

A loss in formal equivalence has been accepted in the target version in favour of a gain in dynamic terms. The translators retell the joke in a completely different way, bearing in mind the lowest common denominator, the invariant core. However, there still remain cases in which the chances of finding an invariant core which is funny in the target language are extremely slim.

21
Q.   How do you make a cat drink?
A.   Easy, put it in a liquidizer.

Come si fa a far bere un gatto?
E' facile, mettilo nel frullatore.

Comment faire boire un chat?
C'est facile, met-le dans le mixer.

These literal translations cannot possibly function as joke forms in Italian or French. In fact, in the two target versions, the utterances become mere exchanges for gaining information. In the English version prominence is given to the item *drink* which leads the recipient to imagine that the answer will have something to do with feeding a feline. The prominence to which the answer alludes is switched to the item *cat*, and produces a rather nasty cocktail. As the Italian and French versions clearly show, syntactic differences in the two translations of 'make someone do something' mean that the same ambiguity cannot be created in the target languages. What is more, *bere* and *boire* are monofunctional and can only function as verbs which precede the noun group *un gatto/un chat*. Thus the target versions are straightforward with no possibility of double-faced puns; they are simply not jokes. (In English, the joke works better in written form since the intonation has to be altered slightly when saying 'cat drink'.)

22

Patient: *I've got a peanut lodged in my throat!*

Doctor: *Then take a cup of drinking chocolate before you go to bed tonight.*

Patient: *Will it get rid of it?*

Doctor: *No, but it'll go down a Treet!*

Italian has no equivalent idiom for 'to go down a treat' and, further-ore, when Treets were on sale in Italy (their name has since been changed to 'M&Ms'), they were known as /trets/ and not /tri:ts/. One alternative open to the translator is to find an Italian product with a linguistically exploitable brand name with which to create a new joke containing a shadow of invariability with the source version. This, however, would be a practical rather than a linguistic solution.

Similarly, Pierino (the stereotypical protagonist of Italian jokes presents a problem as English has no single person who functions as an underdog, e.g. Iaimito, in Spain) goes to the grocer to buy some jam and the grocer asks him if he wants *Arrigoni*, a well-known brand. As *Arrigoni* can be deconstructed to *a rigoni*/'striped', it is only natural that Pierino should refuse and ask for jam which is *a tinta unita* or all one-coloured.

When translating comic plays or films, as we have already seen, it is often preferable to replace a 'difficult' joke with a totally different one in the target language, which, while bearing no relation to the source joke, is, however, obviously a joke in the target version. This may well be preferable to a *non sequitur* or a literal translation plus explanation. By replacing one joke with another, the text still remains a dynamic process. If the joke is to be recited, it may well include a ritualistic element (e.g. riddles, 'knock knock' jokes, etc.) which involves the active participation of the recipient; whether written or oral, the joke will contain a punch which must create a defeat in cultural and/or linguistic expectations. A translation should not ignore such dynamism; therefore substitution with an 'original' target-language joke is more likely to be successful (and run smoothly through the text without jarring) than a faithful, but interactionally poor translation.

Dozens of examples of jokes could be considered and evaluated according to their ease of translatability, but let us return to jokes which do not blatantly play on language. It seems somewhat unfair to suggest that 'prosaic' jokes are not without their problems with regard to translation. While it is evident that heavily language-oriented word play does indeed create peculiar difficulties in translation compared to its less 'poetic' counterparts, it appears to be a question of type of difficulty rather than degree of difficulty.

We cannot claim that some jokes do not play with language, or even that their translation would be any more straightforward than the translation of jokes 18 and 19. Apart from the fact that all jokes depend on language since this is the means by which they are transmitted, such a claim ignores the importance of dynamism which is all-important in a joke.

'Mummy, Mummy, I don't want to go to France!'
'Shut up and keep swimming!'

'Maman, Maman, est-ce que l'Angleterre est loin?'
'Tais-toi et continue à nager!'

Apart from having to substitute England for France, the joke presents no real difficulties to the translator; it does, however, play on language. It forces the recipient to recontextualize the first utterance and in particular the reference of the item *go*. If the joke wanted to be clear (and no longer a joke!) the term *go* could have been replaced with *swim*. Thus, a pretty unambiguous word like 'go' can acquire duplicity from the linguistic environment in which it occurs.

The importance of individual linguistic items in jokes which at first sight do not appear to play with language at all, should not be underestimated. Each element contained within the surface realization acts as a vital catalyst in the joke's dynamic process even if the text does not aim at linguistic exploitation.

The distinction between joke types in prosaic and poetic terms has its limitations, since it overemphasizes the importance of the punch and relegates all the other elements contained in the text to a secondary position, rather than considering that they too are of vital importance to the joke. Attempts at translation show that an unnatural choice in the target version practically anywhere in the text may render a joke a non-starter. The choice of adjective in the following joke, for example, is extremely important in giving it the semblance of a joke rather than an ordinary question. It is the text as whole which creates the joke and not simply a single isolated element.

23
Is rugby a game for men with odd shaped balls?

The tricky part of this translation lies in the substitution for the item *odd*. In Italian, *strano* would appear to be the most obvious choice, yet the effect is itself slightly odd:

Si può dire che il rugby è un gioco con gli uomini con dei palloni strane?

When I tried this out on some native speakers they seemed not to recognize the quip as an attempt at word play. On the other hand, the adjective 'oval'/*ovale(i)* teamed with the item *palle* (rather than *pallone/i* which refers more precisely to a ball used in sports) worked better.

Si può dire che il rugby è un gioco per gli uomini con le palle ovali?

Apart from a preference for the declarative rather than interrogative on the grounds of naturalness within the genre of the Italian aside (the aside has been pre-empted by an interrogative, leaving the joke proper in the declarative to keep some sort of formal equivalence with the source text), the shape adjective preceded by a determiner seems to be a better choice. A French version of the aside is untranslatable, since the word *ballons* can only be used to refer to hollow spheres used in games. However, the same adjectival translation used in the Italian version works in Spanish too:

El Rugby es un juego pala hombres con las pelotas ovalades

However, going back to the Italian, a double-take occurs in this version due to the existence of the idiom *avere le palle quadrate* (literally 'to have square balls'), indicative of a person who is extremely able and astute.

Si può dire che il rugby è un gioco per gli uomini con le palle quadrate?

It is tempting to use this version which is, in fact, more meaningful in Italian than the other versions considered. Unfortunately, however, rugby balls are oval in shape and not square, so the 'ovali' version probably remains the best translation. Interestingly, the target version is more meaningful than the source joke, since rugby is, in fact, played with oval shaped balls, and whether an oval ball is odd or not is merely a question of personal opinion.

As we have seen, in French an invariant core could not be found. In German, too, the word *Bellen*/'balls' cannot refer to parts of the human body, but the joke can work using the word *Eier*, meaning both 'eggs' and an informal variant of the word 'testicles'.

Ist das Rugby ein Spiel für Männer mit seltsam grossen Eiern?

FURTHER CONSIDERATIONS

The Irishman who is transformed into a Belgian and the tightfisted Scot who becomes a Genoese for the benefit of successful translation can be considered surface variants of the same underlying western universal. The introduction of the Italian/Spanish protagonists *Pierino/Iaimito* is a signal to native recipients that they are about to hear a joke. English possesses no such stooge: 'Fred' would not be as effective and 'Paddy' would alter the implications of the source joke. The translator is therefore faced with the choice of leaving such characters unaltered in the target version, or substituting them with more easily recognizable stereotypes specific to the target culture, thus rendering the joke more immediately meaningful. This criterion of meaningfulness is equally valid for any joke, even when content is less 'obvious' than that of, for example, an Irish joke. Just as the experienced translator of literary works rewrites the original, sometimes quite radically, so must the experienced translator of word play totally reformulate and consequently 'retell' a joke *ex novo*.

Every text, whether it is joke or not, will produce a target translation which, by its very nature, will never be quite the same as the source version. Aside from cultural lacunae and linguistic stumbling blocks, a translated joke will tend to be in a language which is, in fact, 'translationese' rather than English, French or whatever target language is required. A translation of some sort is easily, or with difficulty, arrived at eventually, but always with some loss. From the examples considered, it would appear that, in most cases, the best solutions found to overcome difficulties in translation tend to be pragmatic rather than linguistic ones. Replacing an English 'stone' with an Italian 'thrush', or substituting one joke with another, are pragmatic ways out of a linguistic problem.

We have to thus reconsider the issue of impossibility of translation. If we aim at the exact mirroring of discrete items, then translation is indeed out of the question; on the other hand, if we are willing to find a solution such as substitution in functional terms acceptable, then, although not ideal, translation, or rather retelling, is quite feasible.

LANGUAGES IN CONTRAST

A very common type of humour involves jokes which play one language off against another. For example to 'get on', or to 'fare' in Esperanto is *farti*, thus 'How are you' becomes *Kiel vi fartas*? According to teachers of Esperanto, in reply to this greeting it is not at all uncommon for wittily-inclined English speakers to reply with a remark like 'Very loudly'. It would seem that 'false-friends', words in one language which sound like words in another, and which may in some cases be misinterpreted, can also cause laughter. Thus Italians are more than amused by unlikely German expressions such as *Die*

Kätze in der Kühle (meaning 'the cats in the fridge') because *kätze* sounds like the Italian word for 'prick'/*cazzo* and *Kühle* sounds like *culo*/'arse'.

Not at all uncommon are graffiti which are followed by rejoinders in another language. The Scottish camping site which boasts the graffito *Froggies go home!* also possesses the retort *Et ta soeur?* (see p. 80). As we have seen, it is unlikely that the people at whom the retort is aimed will have understood that the innocent sounding comment *Et ta soeur* was meant as a pretty strong insult.

Finally, let us consider the sort of typically English 'intralingual' quip in which Placido Domingo is referred to as *Quiet Sunday*.

NOTES

1 Since going to press the Italian Communist Party no longer exists as such. It has now become the *Partito Democratico di Sinistra*. At present it is still unclear whether *L'Unità* has abandoned its old ideology.
2 This refers to an unofficial translation by Lucia Sinisi and Chris Williams.

5 Word play in action

Jokes, quips and asides do not normally occur in isolation, but as an integrated part of spoken discourse. Consequently, if someone decides to be verbally witty, it is reasonable to suppose that something within the context in which the conversation is taking place has triggered off this desire. Of course, it could equally well be that some element in the preceding discourse has been the cause of a witticism. If humour is generated from some kind of ambiguity, whether verbal or physical, then the prompt for this duplicity is likely to have occurred in the language/social context *around* the example of word play proper. However, although there may be dozens of opportunities in life to pick up on an ambiguous word or situation and joke about it, knowing when it is appropriate to do so is not always easily discernible.

WHEN AND WHERE WORD PLAY IS ACCEPTABLE

While the stage and the television screen create both physical and verbal contexts for well-known comics to display their witty repertoire, the rest of us must rely on invisible antennae, a mixture of instinct and common sense, to tell us when it is safe to joke with someone. Generally speaking, being on friendly terms with people gives us licence to joke verbally at any given moment, while in the case of people with whom we are less well acquainted, play is reserved for conventionally relaxed situations like informal lunches and parties.

More difficult than knowing when to tell a joke proper, is knowing when to make a witty remark or a quip. In Britain it is permissible to play with words in a myriad of situations which are considered out of place in many other cultures, yet knowing when to do so is not solely a cross-cultural problem. It may also happen that our antennae send back the wrong signals when we try to joke with our fellow country-men and women. Most people have at some time or other made what they thought to be a witty remark in the 'wrong' circumstances, only to have then suffered the embarrassment of non-laughter or, worse still, icy glares. Laughing with others is a sign of social acceptance. Unless we know someone extremely well, we may give a polite, albeit false, laugh in response to a witticism which we consider to have been told at the wrong moment, in inappropriate circumstances, or that we do not find particularly funny. Hypocritical as this may appear, it is a social convention. Getting on socially and being polite are a cultural compromise which is generally accepted. Often, witticisms are attempts at establishing a jovial rapport with our interlocutors. Non-laughter on the part of a recipient of a joke may well be interpreted as a signal of social non-acceptance.

When is it, then, that it is perfectly appropriate to tell jokes and play with words? One situation which immediately springs to mind is the joke-capping session in which a number of participants recite joke after joke.

How a joke-capping session begins is hard to say, but frequently something in the preceding discourse serves as a springboard for someone to tell a joke. For example, one participant's account of an event may remind another participant of a similar but humorous event. Once the group begins to laugh, someone else may tell a joke, after which the way is paved for all members present to tell one too. Of course, these sessions do not have to occur in this way; for example, it is not at all unusual for such sessions to begin with someone actually asking the others to tell a joke.

No matter how they begin, what is interesting about joke-capping sessions is that they tend to turn into verbal battles. Each participant tries to outdo the joke told by another participant and, although participants may comment verbally on each joke, laughter is the chief criterion of evaluation. The principal arm in these verbal battles is loudness of voice. Contrary to popular belief, before telling a joke, participants do not necessarily politely ask the others whether they have 'heard the one about . . .', but simply struggle for the floor by shouting above the voices of other participants who are trying to do the same thing.

Joke-capping sessions are particularly useful to the conversational analyst as they reveal several aspects of the rules involved in joke telling. As these sessions contain only jokes, pragmatic rules are easily isolated without the trouble of having to disentangle joke exchanges from the surrounding mass of conversation. The examples which follow are mostly taken from sessions recorded at parties with the participants' knowledge, others were recorded without (although permission to use their conversations was acquired from them later), and others still were jotted down soon after they took place. However, all examples are authentic snippets of genuine conversation.

OPENINGS

Although it is not always the case, someone who is about to tell a joke will often say that they are about to, or will ask permission to do so first. One of the reasons for doing this is, of course, to make sure that the recipient is in the mood to hear a joke; another is to check whether he/she has or has not heard the joke before:

Initiator: *Do you know the one about the Englishman who had an inferiority complex?*
Recipient: No, is it like the architect . . . ?
Initiator: *A little bit like . . .*
Recipient: Oh dear, go on, tell me about the Englishman who had the inferiority complex . . .

In the perpetual fear of the possibility of losing face, initiators seem to require encouragement before embarking on a joke's recital and consequently pre-empt with some sort of face-saving device which distances them from the content of the joke. What is more, a certain amount of negotiation takes place before the joke is actually recited. It is worth noting the recipient's answer to whether or not she has heard the joke: a second request for information which is then followed by an attempt at mitigation by the initiator.

Often a joke will be pre-empted with a request for permission to tell it so as to make sure it will not offend the recipient:

Can I tell you a Spanish joke about Italians?

In this instance, since the joke which followed was rather unkind about Italians, the initiator felt the need to pre-empt it by asking permission first, perhaps out of concern that it might have caused the recipient some offence. The very fact that the question specified that the protagonists of the joke would be Italians seemed to suggest that it might not be to the recipient's liking.

In the next example the speaker wonders if the others are thinking what she is thinking:

John Parrot . . . (pause) . . . someone ought to tell him the parrot joke . . . (pause) . . . have you heard it?

A surname has reminded someone of a joke. As the joke is obscene the initiator does not in fact, as she suggests, tell the joke to the Mr Parrot in question. However, before reciting it to an audience of friends, she makes sure none of them has heard it before.

However, apart from such stock openings, many people will just recite a joke point-blank. This can create pragmatic problems, since the recipient may not have understood that a joke was coming, and this can sometimes be a deliberate ploy on the part of the initiator (see p. 74) who wants to trap her interlocutor into saying something wrong and consequently funny. Nevertheless, normally a joke is pre-empted in some way by the initiator himself. The following sequence, for example, occurred before a feminist joke:

Why are women . . . (pause) . . . here's a sexist joke . . . (pause) . . . why are women bad at parking? It's an incredibly good . . . (pause) bad at parking . . .

Before telling his joke, the man in question evaluates it for his audience. First he warns any women present that it is going to be *sexist* (which is in fact deliberately tricking his audience because it is sexist in an anti-male rather than anti-female way; see p. 8), and then he blows his own trumpet about the quality of the joke which he considers to be *incredibly good*.

Pre-empting with a positive or negative evaluation of the joke about to be told is very frequent. As we have seen, often the person telling the joke does not want to lose face if it falls flat. Thus, warning their audience that it will be qualitatively poor, pre-empting with a distancing evaluation of what is to come, may consequently help them save face. In fact, just in case the joke is not successful, the joker in the next example warns her audience that it is *almost as bad* as the previous joke.

Do you want to hear an Italian joke? It's almost as bad as that one . . .

The following exchange has been extrapolated from a longish joke-capping session. The woman about to tell a joke is worried that her audience will not like it because it follows a string of obscene examples which has put them in a very jovial mood so that their expectations of subsequent jokes are high.

Initiator: What about Mr and Mrs Cauliflower – this isn't rude . . .
Recipient: It's not rude?
Initiator: You don't want it?
Recipient: We don't want it – tell us!

She wants to be sure that her audience is willing to hear a 'clean' joke.

In fact, she interprets her interlocutor's first response – a surprised *It's not rude?* – as disappointment on his part, but, with his next comment – in which he first says he does not want to hear it if it is not 'rude' – we see how he wittily manages to twist the exchange and encourage her to tell the joke. Once more, negotiation has occurred before the telling of a joke.

However, not only the initiator, but recipients too, are free to evaluate an on-coming joke:

Initiator: *What's small and wrinkly and smells of ginger?*
Participant 1: *This is going to be awful . . .*
Participant 2: *. . . a tabby cat's . . .*
Initiator: *I thought this was an old one . . .*

The two participants foresee a punch which is going to be near the knuckle, and participant 2 even tries to guess the answer, but unsuccessfully – at which point the initiator protests about the fact that neither of her interlocutors has actually heard the joke before. In fact, any opening which remotely smacks of bad taste will prompt an evaluation by the recipient:

Initiator: *What's red and sticky and lies in a pram?*
Recipient: *That's horrible!*

Not only do sexual or 'sick' jokes prompt audiences to comment before the punch, but politics, too, is another recipient-sensitive area:

Initiator: *Why is the Tory Party known as the cream of society?*
Participant 1: *I've no idea.*
Participant 2: *I don't think I'm going to like this . . .*

The second participant anticipates that the joke she is about to hear will contain some kind of criticism of the party with which her sympathies lie and voices her predictions.

INTERACTION

Many jokes are so ritualistic that recipients automatically know how to react when faced with an initiation. In the same way as 'knock knock' jokes, riddles too have set interactive rules.

Initiator: *Why is sex like snow?*
Recipient: *I don't know, why is sex like snow?*

The set response to a riddle is to repeat it, optionally pre-empted by something like 'I don't know' or 'I give up'. This repetition functions as a request for an answer. Obviously, the intonation of the response-question is very different from the intonation of the original question:

Initiator: //why is SEX like SNOW?//
//*Recipient:* //I don't know //why IS sex like SNOW?//

The initiator gives prominence to the items *sex* and *snow* because they are the two main content words around which the riddle is constructed; the other items in the question merely function as props for them. The riddler draws attention to *sex* and *snow* as a signal for the recipient to scratch her head and start thinking of common denominators. On the other hand, in the response, prominence is given to the verb *is* which signals a request to the initiator to be told why the two objects are linked.

However, intonation can also be obliquely oriented in the echoed response. This type of intonation occurs when the recipient immediately realizes that she has not heard the riddle before. She thus adopts the ritualistic response without giving much thought to what she is saying. She therefore recites it straight back to the initiator quite flatly:

Initiator: What's the most painful part of a sex change operation?
Recipient: I give up, what's the most painful part of a sex change operation?

What the recipient is saying is of no informative value; it is recited automatically almost like the rote recital of a prayer, football pools results or a mathematical rule. Consequently there is no prominence given to 'new' or 'important' information in the utterance and it acquires an oblique or neutral tone.

SEQUENCING

During joke-capping sessions, jokes are not recited at random but in clusters which are determined either by topic or by joke type. Clear thematic grouping occurs as certain joke types tend to occur in groups; an Irish joke, for example, is likely to spark off a series of Irish jokes, a riddle a series of riddles and so on. In the following transcript of part of a session, a joke about a cauliflower was followed by a joke about another vegetable. This joke was then followed by three obscene jokes which were in turn followed by a joke about a cabbage. The session closed with another obscene joke. What had obviously happened was that the person wanting to tell the third 'vegetable' joke did not manage to gain the floor in time to make his contribution, while the woman telling the dirty jokes was usurped in the process of telling a second one, in rapid succession to the first. As we shall see, clustering relates to both joke type and joke subject matter.

In the transcript, letters indicate different participants. The transcription is as precise as possible but at some points people speak at the same time and overlap each other, thus making understanding impossible. For this reason, I have stated wherever the tape was incomprehensible.

A.   ... er ... did you hear the one about the man ... did you hear about the man ... I saw the other day? He was walking through the streets with a cabbage on the end of a lead and so I went up to him and so I said 'Why've you got a cabbage on the end of that lead? Why're you taking it for a walk?' and he says 'You sure it's a cabbage?' so I says 'Yes' and he said 'The greengrocer lied to me then, he said it was a cauli!'

(laughter)

B.   OK this is cauliflower ...

A.   ... talking about cauliflower ...

B.   There's a cauliflower walking down the street, right ... and he's crossing the road and gets run over ... yes he gets run over and there's bits of cauliflower all over the place, right, so ... er ... the ambulance comes down 'da-da da-da da-da' and takes him to the hospital and then ... em ... his parents are informed ... so Mr and Mrs Cauliflower come along, you know, and they're sort of really nervous in the waiting room ... while he's in intensive care, you know, undergoing surgery and a doctor comes out with a mask over his face and ... you know ... the doctor takes his mask off and says 'I'm sorry to inform you, Mr and Mrs Cauliflower, he's had a few problems and I'm pleased to say, em ... em ... your son ... er ... will live but he'll be a vegetable for the rest of his life.'

(laughter)

A.   How horrible!

B.   Oh dear, never mind, er ...

C.   Can I tell you my one and only joke now?

A.   Go on Sheila.

C.   Why is sex like snow?

A.   ... because ...

Everybody in chorus: We don't know, why is sex like snow?

D.   Let's pretend we don't know ...

C.   Because you never know beforehand how many inches you're gonna get and how long it's gonna last.

A.   That's rude!

D.   Why is Prince Charles' prick blue?

A.   *Because it's always in Di!*
(groan)
D.   *Why do you always groan at my jokes?*
A.   *'cos they're not funny . . .*
B.   *. . . 'cos I heard it yesterday!*
C.   *Why is sex like a bank account?*
A.   *Oh this is for me!*
B.   *Yes.*
C.   *Because as soon as you withdraw you lose interest!*
(laughter)
D.   *Does anybody know any rude ones?*
A.   *er . . . shouldn't think so . . .*
E.   *What's 250 yards long and eats cabbage?*
D.   *What's 250 yards long and eats cabbage?*
E.   *Polish meat queue!*
A.   *That's not rude!*
(laughter)
A.   *There's a rude version of that!*
E.   *What's brown and steams out of cows backwards?*
B.   *I don't know, what's brown and steams out of cows backwards?*
E.   *The Isle of Wight Ferry!*

The two opening 'vegetable' jokes are both similar in structure. They are, in fact, story-style jokes in which the people telling them actually act them out. Participant A recites her story in the first person, while participant B caps it with a convincing performance complete with blowing ambulance siren. Participant C interrupts the possibility of another recital about a vegetable with the question *Why is sex . . . ?* She thus shifts both the topic from cauliflowers to sex and the joke type from narration to riddle. However, before she manages to cap her own joke by reciting a matching riddle – *Why is sex like a bank account?* – participant D comes in with another obscene riddle. The riddle which separates the two *Why is sex like . . . ?* riddles is a variant which has a different structure – *Why is Y's . . . ?*

Interestingly enough, the last 'cabbage' joke – *What's 250 yards long . . . ?* is a riddle too. This time the joke combines the topic which opened the sequence, vegetables, with the frame which had developed out of it, the riddle. While previously vegetables had been presented within the frame of narrative, and sex within the frame of the riddle, now vegetables are being joked about through the question/answer format of the riddle. The final riddle is childishly lavatorial, thus loosely linking back with the three previous, more obscene riddles.

The overall effect of the sequence is one of neat thematic and structural cohesion. See Table 1.

Table 1

Order of joke in conversation	Topic 1	Topic 2	Frame
1	CABBAGE		NARRATIVE
2	CAULIFLOWER		NARRATIVE
3		SEX	RIDDLE (type 1)
4		SEX	RIDDLE (type 2)
5		SEX	RIDDLE (type 1)
6	CABBAGE		RIDDLE (type 3)
7		SCATOLOGY	RIDDLE (type 3)

The next sequence displays similar features regarding thematic grouping:

A.   *Mummy, Mummy, there's a man at the door with a bill! Don't worry chuck, it's probably only a duck with a hat on! (1)*

B.   *. . . (unclear speech) . . . the one about licking the bowl? . . . Mummy, Mummy, can I lick the bowl? (2)*

C.   *No darling, pull the chain like other children.*

A.   *Yes. Mummy, Mummy, can I play with Grandad? No, you've dug him up three times already this week. (3)*

B.   *Mummy, Mummy, what's a vampire? Shut up and eat your soup before it clots! (4)*

C.   *. . . (unclear speech) . . . have to go to France? Shut up and keep swimming! (5)*

D.   *Mummy, Mummy, I don't like Daddy! Leave him on the side of your plate and eat your vegetables. (6)*

E.   *Mummy, Mummy, does the au pair girl come apart? No darling, why do you ask? Because Daddy says he's just screwed the arse off her! (7) . . . How do you make a cat go 'woof'? (8)*

A.   *Dunno. How do you make a cat go 'woof'?*

E.   *Douse it in paraffin, chuck it on the fire and it goes 'woooof'!*

A.   *How do you make a dog go 'Miaow'? (9)*

C.   *What's red and sticky and lies in a pram? (10)*

A.   *That's horrible!*
C.   *A baby with a razor blade.*
A.   *How do you make a dog go 'Miaow'?*
E.   *Dunno. How do you make a dog go 'Miaow'?*
A.   *Tie its tail to the back of Concorde and it goes 'Miaaaaow'.*
E.   *How do you make a cat drink?*
A.   *A cat drink?*
E.   *Yeah.*
A.   *Dunno. How do you make a cat drink?*
E.   *Put it in a liquidizer.*

The first six jokes, which are recited in rapid succession, are all structured around a 'Mummy, Mummy' frame. Each pseudo-dialogue is capped by another until at the eighth joke we get a rather sick riddle about a dog. Influenced by the *How do you make a cat . . . ?* joke, participant A next takes the floor and begins to recite a matching riddle about a dog, but he is interrupted by participant C who manages to cap it with a sick riddle about a baby. Not only does this riddle create a shift in topic but also in riddle type. Instead of *How do you make . . . ?* we have *What's X and Y and . . . ?* Once participant C has told her joke, participant A regains the floor and this time is encouraged through participant E's response to ask her joke about the dog. Participant E closes the sequence with another sick cat joke which matches the other two animal jokes, i.e. *How do you make a cat/dog + verb?*

Once the participants had run out of 'Mummy, Mummy' jokes, they quickly replaced them with a group of ritualistic riddles with the result of both thematic and structural clustering. See Table 2.

It is interesting to note how thematic similarity occurs. It would seem to be sufficient for someone to hear a word remotely connected with another to trigger off a joke containing elements from the same lexical field. Notice in the next sequence how the word *constipation* triggers off two other jokes loosely connected with health.

Initiator: *Did you hear what happened to the mathematician with CONSTIPATION? He sat down and worked it out with a pencil!*
Participant 1: *That's an old one.*
Participant 2: *That reminds me, the DR FINLAY jokes, 'DR CAMERON, why are you writing with an ANAL THERMOMETER?' 'Some BUM's got my pencil jammed up it!'*
(laughter)
Participant 3: *. . . (unclear speech) . . . out of AIDS, SYPHILIS, HERPES, Skoda and a Barratts House?*
Initiator: *I don't know.*

Table 2

Order of joke in conversation	Topic	Frame
1	SILLY MISUNDERSTANDING	'MUMMY, MUMMY'
2	TOILETS	'MUMMY, MUMMY'
3	NECROPHILIA	'MUMMY, MUMMY'
4	CANNIBALISM	'MUMMY, MUMMY'
5	ABSURD TASK	'MUMMY, MUMMY'
6	CANNIBALISM	'MUMMY, MUMMY'
7	SEX	'MUMMY, MUMMY'
8	CAT	RIDDLE
9	SADISM (?)	RIDDLE
10	DOG	RIDDLE
11	CAT	RIDDLE

Participant 3:   *SYPHILIS 'cos it's the only one you can get rid of!*
Initiator: *Why do BEES hum?*
Participant 3:   *Because . . .*
Participant 1:   *Is that it?*
Initiator: *It's quite old, it's quite nostalgic that . . . what's the last thing to go through a BLUEBOTTLE'S mind as it hits the windscreen of a car?*
Participant 1:   *I don't know.*
Participant 2:   *Dunno. The wipers?*
Initiator: *It's ARSE!*

The word *constipation* in the initiator's one-liner prompted participant 2 to recite a 'medically' oriented Dr Finlay joke and participant 3 to tell a modern-day *Which is the odd one out?* riddle, in which syphilis is seen as the best of several evils. The initiator then shifts the topic to a traditional riddle involving bees, which then reminds him of yet another concerning an insect, this time a fly. The punch of the final joke includes an anatomical reference which links it back to the first two jokes in the chunk of conversation.

Quite unconsciously the people taking part in this conversation have created a stretch of spoken text which coheres perfectly. It opens with *constipation* and closes with *arse*. In between we find other words pertaining to the same anatomical area, i.e. *bum* and *anal*. Apart from the three diseases, *aids*, *syphilis*, *herpes*, the 'medical' jargon is juxtaposed with a brief entomological interlude involving a *bee* and a *bluebottle*.

Initiator → CONSTIPATION   (joke 1)

Participant 2 → DR FINLAY → DR CAMERON → ANAL THERMOMETER → BUM   (joke 2)

Participant 3 → AIDS → SYPHILIS → HERPES   (joke 3)
Participant 3 → SYPHILIS

Initiator → BEES   (joke 4)

Initiator → BLUEBOTTLE   (joke 5)
↓
ARSE

EVALUATION

Someone decides to tell a joke and, we hope, the audience will laugh. Of course, there may be an interval before the joke is actually told because the initiator may want to make sure that the recipients have not heard the joke before or that it will not offend them; thus, after negotiation, laughter should follow – *should* because if the joke is an old one or the pun excruciating, it may well be followed by a groan. However, whether through laughter or a groan, the joke will be evaluated.

The dynamics of joke interaction

1 PRE-EMPTING/NEGOTIATION
(e.g. A. Sh . . . Sh . . . can I do my skinhead one?
B. Go on then . . .
A. It's really quite sweet . . .)

2 OPENING
(e.g. Do you know the one about . . .)

3   JOKE
(e.g. Why did the chicken cross the road . . .)

4   INTERACTION (optional)
(e.g. I don't know, what is the difference between a light bulb and a pregnant woman?)

5   RECITAL OF JOKE

6   LAUGHTER/GROANS and/or VERBAL EVALUATION

The flow diagram illustrates the typical dynamics of a speech event in which a joke is told. The joke may be preceded by an utterance which serves to reassure the initiator, or it may be preceded by a sort of pre-exchange, after which the joke is presented, told, interacted with and finally evaluated. Frequently, however, together with, or instead of, laughter or a groan, verbal evaluation will occur in the form of some kind of comment regarding the recipient's opinion of the joke. In fact, what occurs most commonly is the concurrence of laughter and/or groans plus a verbal comment.

The quickest way to make the initiator of a joke lose face is to withhold laughter, or, worse still, not to comment at all. A final evaluation seems not only to tie up the loose ends of the speech event, but also to encourage the joker.

Initiator: *Why is sex like a bank account?*
                Because when you withdraw you lose interest!
Participant 1: *That's good!*
Participant 2: *That's . . . (unclear) . . .*
Participant 3: *That's very good, I like that.*
Initiator: *Yes.*

This particular joke prompts three positive evaluations plus a self-satisfied evaluation from the initiator herself; but, of course, not all jokes are so successful:

Initiator: *Why is the Tory party known as the cream of society?*
Participant 1: *I've no idea!*
Participant 2: *I don't think I'm going to like this.*
Initiator: *Because it's rich and thick and full of clots!*
Participant 3: *Ha, ha, ha. Not very good.*
Participant 1: *I like it.*

The initiator of the 'Tory' joke loses face slightly because of participant 3's sarcastic *Ha, ha, ha* followed by a straightforward negative evaluation. While participant 2 passes no comment since she has already warned the initiator that she does not expect the joke to be to her taste, participant 1 closes the exchange with an appraisal.

The next exchange illustrates how an unexpected punchline can both please and disappoint different recipients:

Initiator: *What's green with 22 balls and 6 brown legs and if it fell out of a tree would kill you?*

Participant 1:. . . green, 22 balls and 6 brown legs . . .

Participant 2:. . . 6 legs and 22 balls . . .

Initiator: *A snooker table!*

Participant 1: How clever!

Participant 2: Disappointing!

The response which so disappoints participant 2 renders the joke *clever* to participant 1. Clearly, the comment *Disappointing* reveals that one recipient had expected a more obscene answer. The point of the riddle was indeed to trick recipients into expecting an obscene solution, which is precisely why participant 1 sees it as being a 'clever' joke.

Just as an initiator may pre-empt the quality of the joke she is about to tell, so may she also comment on it after it has been told:

Initiator: *. . . Have you ever kissed a parrot?*

Audience: *No.*

Initiator: *But I bet you've kissed a cock-a-too!*
(laughter)
Whenever I hear the word 'parrot' now I must tell that joke!
(laughter)

A participant: That's wonderful, I like that!

This joke occurred in informal company but on a fairly formal occasion. The initiator seems to be trying to justify her witty outburst and to explain why a joke should cross her mind on such an occasion. Audience evaluation closes the exchange.

'PING-PONG PUNNING'

What occurs during a joke-capping session is extremely convenient for the analyst. If he happens to have a tape recorder on him, he will be able to record a good number of jokes and examine pragmatic features such as openings, closures and interaction without having to deal with the intrusion of any discourse which is non-humorous. However, joke-capping sessions are not an everyday occurrence and when they do occur it is probably fair to say that they are not necessarily indicative of where, when and how jokes normally happen. Furthermore joke-capping sessions, as the label suggests, specialize in jokes, while it is likely that word play will more often occur within the bounds of an everyday conversation, the aim of which is not to tell jokes.

Joke-capping sessions are competitive manifestations of feats of memory. As far as linguistic events go, they are indeed odd. In a certain sense, no new information is actually communicated as in 'normal' transformational discourse (unless we consider each quip or story as world-changing pieces of information for its recipients), nor is the interaction which takes place merely phatic. Each participant in such an event is showing off verbally and demonstrating her cleverness while at the same time evaluating the repertoire of fellow participants. A joke-capping session can best be compared to a verbal game like rapping, in which topping or capping through the quality of jokes substitutes for the adjectival capping of the rap.

Outside such sessions, a joke or aside is likely to disrupt a 'normal' or 'serious' conversation (i.e. a conversation which is not composed solely of jokes). Evaluation following the joke, whether verbal or non-verbal, will distract participants from whatever discourse had preceded the witty interruption. It is also fairly likely that the joke will provoke a chain reaction by subconsciously inviting others to follow suit with a recital of their own jokes. An exchange made up mainly of jokes is thus born, serious interaction breaks down and humorous discourse replaces it.

However, humorous discourse is not only made up of a stretch of conversation made up of strings of jokes. Another form of comic discourse may occur in the form of what can be described as 'ping-pong-punning'. 'Ping-pong-punning' is a term used to describe what happens when the participants of a conversation begin punning on every possible item in each other's speech which may contain the slightest ambiguity. A game (or battle) comparable to ping-pong in which each participant tries to outdo the others' cleverness results. This form of word play probably occurs more frequently than full-blown joke-capping sessions.

The next two examples are interludes which occurred within a joke-capping session and illustrate this type of word play. The participants move away from the crescendo of jokes being recited and begin to concentrate on a more interactive form of joking.

Initiator: What's small and wrinkled and smells of ginger?
Participant 1: This is going to be awful . . .
Participant 2: . . . a tabby cat's . . .

Initiator: *Fred Astaire's cock.*
Participant 1: *It's an old one!*
Participant 2: *1930!*

Participant 1's evaluation was certainly referring to the joke and not to part of the famous tap-dancer's anatomy; she had heard the joke before and obviously found it distasteful. On hearing the punchline, participant 2 immediately picks up on the ambiguity of *one* and plays on it by punning on the man's, and consequently his anatomy's, age. The whole exchange coheres perfectly and the previous discourse is replaced by the cohesive coherence of the new humorous stretch of discourse.

Initiator: *What's the last thing that goes through a bluebottle's mind as it*
                hits the windscreen of a car?
Participant 1: *I don't know.*
Participant 2: *Dunno. The wipers?*
Initiator: *It's arse!*
Participant 1: *Cruel. I'm a bluebottleist myself.*
Participant 2: *No flies on you Sheila!*

Together with her evaluation, the first participant invents a nonce-term, *bluebottleist*, to demonstrate wittily her disapproval of the joke. This remark is then picked up by the other participant who throws the ball back into her court by topping the portmanteau with an idiom which includes the term *flies*. Here too, the text coheres smoothly.

It should, however, be pointed out that exchanges of ping-pong-punning do not necessarily stem from jokes, nor do they only occur in joke-capping sessions. In fact, such instances of punning tend to stem from more serious utterances. Consider the following exchange which was prompted by someone who had their arm in plaster:

Initiator: *No 'arm in it, eh Peter?*
Participant: *Yeah, got to hand it to you . . .*
Peter: *That's not funny!*
Initiator: *Put my finger on it have I?*
Participant: *'armless enough!*

The exchange revolves around four idioms which can all be seen to joke on Peter's injured limb. The initiator starts punning and the other participant puns straight back at him. Peter's appeal for a truce is taken as a signal to continue battling. The concatenation of puns stems from an initial pun on *harm/arm* which generates punning on the items *finger* and *hand*.

Possibly better examples of this type of interaction stem from an unambiguous item which crops up within a conversation. Ping-pong-punning is frequently reported by the writer of popular romances, Jilly Cooper. In her novels, characters will tend to be brought together at dinner parties at which she allows them to practise witty repartee:

'Hi Jake. Congratulations. I was so excited when I heard you were in.'

'As the actress said to the Bishop,' said Rupert. 'You're priveleged, Jake. You must be the only person who's excited my dear wife in years. I certainly don't.'

(*Riders*, p. 494)

Rupert takes his wife's congratulatory remark at face value and 'frames' it in music-hall style, 'As the actress said to the bishop . . .' – a classic frame for sexual innuendo, to bring out the *double entendre*. Furthermore he also picks up on the double meaning of the item *excited*. Similarly, in real life we find the following exchange:

Participant A:. . . you have to see the arras.
Initiator: (giggles) such a lovely ar-ras [/ə:s/]
(laughter)
Participant B:Has it got a hole in it?

In the middle of a serious conversation on art someone finds the word *arras* reminiscent of the word *arse*, corrupts it to the target word, which in turn prompts another participant to joke about it too. In this way the same joke is developed and expanded as it crosses single-speaker boundaries.

In the next example, something similar occurs: a participant in a conversation hardly manages to gain the floor, when she is interrupted by a pun generated from the topic on which she was about to speak.

Participant A:Our farmer
Participant B:Who art in heaven . . .

During a conversation about a car accident, drivers were said to be 'weaving' through the traffic, at which the participant concerned protested that

I wasn't weaving, I was knitting.

This particular remark simply disrupts the prior conversation which is then replaced by laughter.

Sometimes, a whole utterance in a conversation, as opposed to a single item, is picked up and joked upon. Consider the following example which cropped up in a recording of a dinner party:

A. *I can't remember the last time I was on a London bus . . .*
B. *Think of a conversation leading up to that remark.*

Participant B's comment disrupts the flow of conversation by provoking a great deal of laughter. What he has done is to decontextualize A's comment, thus depriving it of any coherence with regard to the surrounding conversation, and attempt to stimulate the other participants' imaginations by encouraging them to think of another, perhaps more humorous context, in which it may have occurred.

HUMOROUS DISCOURSE VERSUS SERIOUS DISCOURSE

The types of humorous discourse examined so far – joke-capping sessions and stretches and 'ping-pong-punning' – could well be seen as rather extreme habitats in which jokes may occur. Artificial situations such as the screen, the stage and books possibly contain equally unusual occurrences of word play too, especially if we consider the quantity and density of jokes and quips humorous films and plays may contain. In real life, jokes may, of course, occur anywhere and at any moment. Furthermore, they do not always necessarily generate other jokes. Convenient as stretches of jokes may be for analysis, most jokes probably do indeed occur in isolation. It is also worth bearing in mind that humorous discourse does not only occur in joke form, nor as punning or quipping. The narration of amusing events and comic anecdotes is also part of the comic mode.

Jokes and quips, as we have seen, can interrupt serious conversation, as can ping-pong-punning. Both phenomena may provoke a chain reaction which will allow other participants to follow suit and recite their own jokes or puns, so that an interlude of humorous discourse replaces the serious discourse which had been going on previously. The same thing occurs when someone tells a funny story; thematic grouping is such that funny stories tend to occur together. Someone who tells an amusing tale is likely to cause someone else to follow suit.

Participant A:Do you know that there's a factory between Rome and Naples called 'Arsole'? It's spelt A-R-S-O-L-E.
Participant B:And . . . and Delia laughs every time we go by it on the train and the whole train turns round . . .
Participant C:. . . Genoa . . . c'è una scritta cubitale: F-A-R-T.
[In Genoa there's a neon sign which spells out 'Fart']

Participant B:E la gente che fa . . . ubbidisce? [does everyone obey?] Oh
  look! Genoa . . . it gives a whole new dimension to the Achille
  Lauro!

The participants, who all speak fluent English and Italian, code-switch continually and with ease, picking up on accidental meanings which do not exist in the reciprocal source languages (see Chapter 4). Participant A sets out by narrating something which she considers funny. Participant C recounts a similar example, while Participant B expands and jokes upon the last 'story'.

Seen in these terms it would seem that humorous discourse and serious discourse are two discourse types which are neatly separated from one another. However, if we examine matters more closely, we find that on the interface between serious and humorous discourse there lies a whole shady area of discourse which can be defined either by both or by neither of the two terms. Real-life stories can, of course, be narrated in more than one way. Depending on the stance the narrator wishes to take, the verbalization of a single event can present a very different aspect, depending upon whether it is told seriously or humorously.

Let us consider the following transcription of a story narrated during a dinner party:

I went to Florence one very hot weekend in June and, as I was walking around waiting for the appointments I had, I thought I'd go and buy some talcum powder to dry myself out a bit and then to find somewhere . . . to go . . . and put it on. After a while I came to a bookshop so I asked where the English books were and they told me they were upstairs. So I trotted upstairs and, when I got there, there was a young boy who was looking at some books and he eventually left so I was left alone on the upstairs floor so I thought that that was a good moment to put my talcum powder on. So there I was shooshing [sic] talcum powder down my blouse, up my skirt etcetera. Finally, I felt better, chose my books, walked downstairs. When I went to pay at the cash desk I saw that they had a closed circuit television camera which had been pointed exactly where I'd been sitting and all the staff were standing around the television camera. I've never been so embarrassed in my whole life. I went bright red, paid and rushed out of the shop and I shall never go there again.

What happened to the lady concerned understandably caused her acute embarrassment. However, she chooses to recount her experience in a humorous, rather than a serious fashion. The event itself is indeed funny. We tend to laugh at people who make fools of themselves and lose face, and, here, the narrator plays the role of the 'fool' who joins in with her audience by poking fun at herself.

How is it that she renders the event amusing? Interestingly enough, in this text, the speaker's intonation is deadly serious, at least at the beginning. Perhaps this is some sort of subconscious interactive ploy to trick her audience and thus render the 'punch' – when she realizes that she has been seen by several people with her blouse undone and skirt up – even more surprising and consequently funnier. However, she only starts being funny at the word *trotted*, not a word one would normally use to render the meaning of 'to go upstairs' unless one wanted to add some kind of comic texture to what one was saying. In this case, the choice of item changes the tone of the text and begins to render it lighter. The speaker also adopts the nonce-term *shooshing* which conveys the idea of someone covering themselves with clouds of talc perfectly. Furthermore, the speaker uses euphemisms such as . . . *to dry myself out* . . .; and listeners are left to work out for themselves what 'etcetera' might stand for.

Discourse markers are of an informal variety too. Consider the effect of the syntactic inversion of *So there I was shooshing myself with talcum powder* . . . as opposed to something like 'I was using the talcum powder to cool myself a little . . .'. Consider also the matching pair *down my blouse and up my skirt*. Of course, intonation, gesture and comic expressions add to the overall comic effect; the speaker deliberately stresses the items *all* and *exactly*, thus turning them into intensifiers. The whole text is exaggerated and almost hyperbolic. To render it serious the text would need to be 'toned down' and 'formalized' by substituting the words and expressions used with more neutral, more denotative ones.

It is worth noting, however, that the narrator knew beforehand that she was being recorded, which may be the reason for the unusually neat ending, complete with an implicit moral; she obviously felt that the story had to have a formal ending.

The following account of a road accident is reported below in two versions; an inflated, comic version and a serious version.

Version 1

1　*So there I was lying in hospital . . . all my ribs broken, collar bone*
2　*broken, no knee left and my face all scarred when my stomach started*
3　*to swell! Well . . . all these doctors round my bed talking about peritoni-*
4　*tis . . . I suppose they thought I was stupid or something and couldn't*
5　*understand what they meant! Anyhow, they told me I had to have a*
6　*sonda rettale.* Well . . . have you ever seen a sonda rettale? It's a piece*

* *An anal probe.*

7　*of rubber tubing about this long . . . (gesticulation) . . . well . . . along*
8　*comes this nurse . . . and I couldn't move you see . . . 'cos all me ribs*
9　*were broken and I had to lie flat . . . and she starts fiddling about*
10　*somewhere in my lower regions. After a few minutes she looks up and*
11　*says: 'I'm afraid you'll have to do it yourself, signorina, because I can't*
12　*find the right hole!'*

Version 2
I was lying in bed with all my ribs broken, a broken collar bone and apparently a totally smashed up rotula. I was in a dreadful state when my stomach began to swell visibly. What was particularly frightening was that the doctors stood round my bed and talked about the chances of my having contracted peritonitis in front of me! The situation was terrifying enough as it was, but I got more frightened still when I was told I would have to have a sonda rettale. In order to distract me while a nurse started inserting the rubber tube, a doctor gave me a few extra stitches on my left knee. Funnily enough, it wasn't as painful as I thought . . . and no wonder . . . the nurse didn't know how to insert the tube and asked me to do it myself.

The first version is funny. The narrator seems to have a preference for the anecdotal style marker: *So there I was* . . . ; the style is informal, with a marked absence of finite verbs (lines 1 to 3). This is a particularly common feature of informal story telling in English. The story is acted 'up' as the narrator interacts with her audience and asks for their reactions: *Well, have you ever seen a . . .?* The style is casual and chatty (e.g. *you see* and the use of the personal pronoun *me* instead of 'my' and the contracted *'cos*). The casualness reaches its climax with the nurse's comment, introduced, once more, with an anecdotal use of the present tense: *she says* instead of a more formal 'she said'. Finally, the story is topped by the choice of lexis for the voicing of the nurse's fears; she does not want, in fact, to insert the probe in the euphemistic, brutal yet comic *wrong hole*.

The second version is less dramatic, more objective and more formal. Apart from the syntactic correctness of the text, which could just as easily have been written as told, feelings are described in subdued terms without the emotional involvement of her listeners. By 'playing down' lexical choices the serious version of what had previously been told humorously is obtained.

A division between serious and humorous discourse is not always so clear-cut, so it would perhaps be more exact to consider these two labels as the poles of a cline. If at one pole we find word play, in terms of unexpected occurrences of paradigmatic choices, and at the other pole clearly referential uses of language, in the centre we find a vast zone which belongs to neither pole, yet at the same time has many points in common with both. Humorous stories are good examples of the point at which the two poles meet.

Conclusion

To echo the words of Samuel Beckett, 'In the beginning there was the pun' (*Murphy*).

It would indeed appear that all natural languages contain ambiguities which can be deliberately exploited to create verbal duplicity, yet, as has been suggested in this book, word play may well be more pervasive in Britain than elsewhere. The exclusiveness of humorous discourse to those who are part of a particular group of people can easily create a barrier between those who are unaware of the complexity and quantity of linguistic options available to the punster. Despite the fact that English has now become an international language, its expressions of humour remain a mystery to all but its most proficient speakers. What is more, in British society, verbal play tends to be ubiquitous. It seems to be acceptable to play with words in a myriad of situations in which it would be considered out of place in many other cultures. Thus a foreigner could be confused by the occurrence of a joke, or else find that his attempt at punning is met with disapproval, not only because he has chosen the wrong moment or place to play with words, but above all because his audience is unwilling to accept him as part of their 'group'.

Nowadays the teaching of English as a foreign language embraces practice in several linguistic skills and sub-skills, while at the same time it develops the appreciation of literature. Word play could provide both teachers and learners with a wealth of authentic material which, as well as being readily available, could also be enjoyable once made accessible. Such accessibility does not come naturally. The foreign speaker needs to be guided towards the understanding and subsequently the appreciation of British humour. Furthermore, a knowledge of British humour and its pervasiveness is a central part of British culture, possibly more important, for example, than a national preference for tea over coffee. Yet, while learners of English are forced to learn about the importance of tea and fish and chips they are very rarely exposed to examples of English humour.

This book presents a brief overview of verbal play in English and has touched upon various aspects of the subject. If we are willing to accept that word play can be considered a form of 'layman's poetry', then what has transpired is that playing with language can bring out the poetic side of the layperson who is able to distort words and texts and thus manipulate that multifaceted entity which is the English language. The form of 'poetry' – jokes – which is generated by these 'poets' is accessible to anyone who understands the language and the culture. Not only are the authors of these texts comic poets, but they are also actors who through their use of accent, pauses and timing often produce magnificent performances in which weak jokes can be transformed into everyday but none the less noteworthy master-pieces.

Bibliography

Alexander, R. J. (1978; 1979) 'Fixed expressions in English: a linguistic, psycholinguistic, sociolinguistic and didactic study', *Anglistik und Anglischunterricht* 6, pp. 171–88; 7, pp. 181–202.

Alexander, R. J. (1980) 'English verbal humour and second language learning', *Laut Paper*, Series B, no. 60, University of Trier.

Alexander, R. J. (1981) *British Comedy and Humour. Social and Cultural Background*, University of Brema.

Alexander, R. J. (1981) 'A linguistic angle on English jokes: humour material for advanced English training', *Beiträge zur Fremsprachen vermittlung aus dem Konstanzer SLI* 9, pp. 3–16.

Alexander, R. J. (1982) 'Verbal humour: its implications for the second language learner and teacher', *Grazer Linguistiche Studien* 17/18.

Alexander, R. J. (1982) 'What's in a four-letter word? Its implications for the second language learner and teacher', *Die Neueren Sprachen* 81, pp. 219–24.

Alexander, R. J. (1983) 'Catch phrases rules OK: allusive puns analysed', *Grazer Linguistiche Studien* 20, pp. 2–31.

Alexander, R. J. (1983) 'Metaphors, connotations, allusions: thoughts on the language-culture connection in learning English as a foreign language', *Laut Paper*, Series B, no. 9 University of Trier.

Alexander, R. J. (1985) 'Doing it in a manner of speaking: investigations into a punner's plaything', *Grazer Linguistiche Studien* 25.

Aristotle (1927) *Poetics*, trans. Hamilton Fyfe, London, Heinemann.

Attridge, D. (1982) *The Rhythms of English Poetry*, Harlow, Longman.

Austin, J. L. (1962) *How to do Things with Words*, Oxford, Clarendon Press.

Bassnett-McGuire, S. (1980) *Translation Studies*, London, Methuen.

Bergson, H. (1900) *Le Rire: Essai sur la signification du comique*, Paris, Alcan.

Bier, J. (1979) 'Humor and social change in twentieth century America', Boston, Public Library of the City of Boston.

Bier, J. (1988) 'The problem of the Polish joke', *Humor* 1–2.

Bolinger, D. (1968) *Aspects of Language*, New York, Harcourt Brace Jovanovich.

Bolinger, D. (1970) 'Getting the words in', *American Speech* 45, pp. 78–85.

Brazil, D. C., Coulthard, R. M. and Johns, C. M. (1980) *Discourse Intonation and Language Teaching*, London, Longman.

Brazil, D. C., (1985) *The Communicative Value of Intonation in English*, Birmingham, Birmingham University English Language Research.

Carroll, L. (1982) *Alice's Adventures in Wonderland and through the Looking Glass*, Oxford, Oxford University Press.

Cicero (1965) *De Oratore, libri tres*, Hidesheim, Olm.

Coulthard, R. M. (1977) *An Introduction to Discourse Analysis*, London, Longman.

de Beaugrande, R. (1978) *Factors in a Theory of Poetic Translation*, Amsterdam and Assen, Van Gorcum.

Derrida, J. (1968) 'Grammatologie et sémiologie', *Informations sur les Sciences Sociales* 7, pp. 135–48.

de Saussure, F. (1974) *Course in General Linguistics*, London, Fontana.

Eisiminger, S. (1979) 'Colourful Language', *Verbatim*, Vol. VI, no. 1, pp. 1–3.

Farb, P. (1974) *Word Play. What Happens When People Talk*, London, Jonathan Cape.

Fernando, C. and Flavell, R. (1981) *On Idiom. Critical Views and Perspectives*, Exeter, University of Exeter Press.

Firth, J. R. (1957) *Papers in Linguistics, 1934–1951*, London, Oxford University Press.

Freud, S. (1976) *Jokes and their Relation to the Subconscious*, Harmondsworth, Penguin.

Grice, H. P. (1975) 'Logic and conversation', in Cole, P. and Morgan, J. L. (eds), *Syntax and Semantics III: Speech Acts*, New York, Academic Press, pp. 41–55.

Halliday, M. A. K. (1973) *Explorations in the Functions of Language*, London, Edward Arnold.

Halliday, M. A. K. (1975) *Learning How to Mean*, London, Edward Arnold.

Halliday, M. A. K. (1976) 'Types of process', in Kress, G., *System and Function in Language*, London, Oxford University Press, pp. 159–73.

Halliday, M. A. K. and Hasan, R. (1976) *Cohesion in English*, London, Longman.

Halliday, M. A. K. (1978) *Language as Social Semiotic*, London, Edward Arnold.

Hockett, C. F. (1967) 'Where the tongue slips there slip I', in *To Honour Roman Jakobson*, Vol. II, The Hague, Mouton.

Hockett, C. F. (1977) 'Jokes', in *The View from Language: Selected Essays 1948–1964*, Athens, Georgia, pp. 257–89.

Hoey, M. (1983) *On the Surface of Discourse*, Allen & Unwin, London.

Hymes, D. (1972) 'On communicative competence', in Pride, J. B. and Holmes, J. (eds), *Sociolinguistics*, Harmondsworth, Penguin, pp. 269–85.

Jacobson, S. (1975) 'Chelsea Rule – O.K.', *New Society* 20 March.

Jakobson, R. (1959) 'On linguistic aspects of translation', in R. A. Browes (ed.), *On Translation*, Cambridge, Mass., Harvard University Press.

Kelly, L. G. (1971) 'Punning and the linguistic sign', *Linguistics* 66, pp. 5–11.

Koestler, A. (1974) 'Humour and wit', in *Encyclopaedia Britannica*, Vol. 9, Chicago, Benton, pp. 5–11.

Kristeva, J. (1968) 'Poésie et négativité, in *L'Homme* 8, pp. 36–63.

Kristeva, J. (1970) *Le Texte du roman*, The Hague and Paris, Mouton.

La Fave, L., Hadda, J. and Maessens, W. A. (1976) 'Superiority, enhanced self-esteem and perceived incongruity humour theory', in Chapman,

A. G. and Foot, H. C. (eds), *Humour and Laughter: Theory, Research and Applications*, London, pp. 63–91.

Lakoff, R. (1969) 'Some reasons why there can't be any *some any* rule', *Language* 45, pp. 608–15.

Lausberg, H. (1967) *Elemente der literarichten Rhetorik*, Munich, Max Hueber Verlag.

Leech, G. N. (1966) *English in Advertising: A Linguistic Study of Advertising in Great Britain*, London, Longman.

Leech, G. N. (1969) *A Linguistic Guide to English Poetry*, London, Longman.

Leech, G. N. (1974) *Semantics*, Harmondsworth, Penguin.

Lefevere, A. (1975) *Translating Poetry, Seven Strategies and a Blueprint*, Amsterdam, Van Gorcum.

Lyons, J. (1963) *Structural Semantics*, Oxford, Blackwell.

Lyons, J. (1977) *Semantics*, Vol. II, Cambridge, Cambridge University Press.

Makkai, A. (1972) *Idiom Structure in English*, The Hague, Mouton.

McLean, A. (1974) 'Make 'em laugh: the lesson of TV comedy', *Educational Broadcasting International* 7/1, pp. 14–16.

Milner, G. B. (1972) 'Homo ridens: towards a semiotic theory of humour and laughter', *Semiotica* 5, pp. 1–28.

Nash, W. (1985) *The Language of Humour*, London, Longman.

Nida, E. (1964) *Toward a Science of Translating*, Leiden, E. J. Brill.

Norrick, N. R. (1981) 'Proverbial linguistics: linguistic perspectives on proverbs', *Laut Paper*, Series B, no. 69, University of Trier.

Opie, I. and Opie, P. (1959) *The Language and Lore of Schoolchildren*, London, Oxford University Press.

Palmer, F. R. (1976) *Semantics* (second edition), Cambridge, Cambridge University Press.

Plato (1925) *Philebus*, ed. Harold N. Fowler, London, Heinemann.

Popovic, A. (1976) *Dictionary for the Analysis of Literary Translation*, Edmonton, Alberta, Department of Comparative Literature, University of Alberta.

Quirk, R., Greenbaum, S., Leech, G. and Svartvik, J. (1972) *A Grammar of Contemporary English*, Harlow, Longman.

Redfern, W. (1984) *Puns*, Oxford, Basil Blackwell.

Sacks, H. (1967–1971) *Mimeo Lecture Notes*.

Sacks, H. (1970 and 1971) *Studies in the Organization of Conversational Interaction* (unpublished mimeographs) 1–8, 1970 and 1–16, 1971.

Sacks, H. (1972) 'On the analysability of stories by children', in Gumperz, J. J. and Hymes, D., *Directions in Sociolinguistics*, New York, Holt Rinehart and Winston.

Sacks, H., Schegloff, E. A. and Jefferson, G. (1974) 'A simplest systematics for the organization of turn-taking in conversation', *Language* 50/4, pp. 696–735.

Sherzer, J. (1978) 'Oh! That's a pun and I didn't mean it', *Semiotica* 22, 3/4.

Sinclair, J. and Coulthard, R. M. (1975) *Towards an Analysis of Discourse*, London, Oxford University Press.

Sopher, H. (1981) 'Laugh and learn', *English Language Teaching Journal* 35, pp. 431–6.

Strawson, P. F. (1964) 'Intention and convention in speech acts', *Philosophical Review* 73, pp. 439–60.

Vizmuller, J. (1979/80) 'Psychological reasons for using humour in a pedagogical setting', *Canadian Modern Language Review* 36, pp. 266–71.

White, D. (1979) 'The funny side of advertising', *New Society*, 4 October.

Whorf, B. L. (1956) *Language, Thought and Reality* (Selected Writings), ed. J. B. Carroll, Cambridge, Mass., MIT Press.

Wilson, C. P. (1979) *Jokes*, London, Academic Press.

Winter, E. O. (1977) 'A clause-relational approach to English texts', *Instructional Science* 6, 1.

Zhao, Y. (1988) 'The information-conveying aspect of jokes', *Humor*, Vols 1–3, Berlin, Mouton.

Zijderveld, A. D. (1979) *On Clichés*, London, Routledge & Kegan Paul.

SOURCES FOR EXAMPLES

Acquisti, D. (1982) *Le barzellette di Pierino*, Roma, Napoleone.

Ash, R. (1983) *The Cynic's Dictionary*, London, Corgi.

Barker, R. and Corbett, R. (1978) *The Bumper Book of the Two Ronnies*, London, Star.

Brandreth, G. (1980) *1000 Riddles, The Greatest Book of Riddles Ever Known*, London, Carousel.

Brandreth, G. (1985) *1000 Word Wonders*, London, Carousel.

Cohen, J. M. (1975) *A Choice of Comic and Curious Verse*, Harmondsworth, Penguin.

Cooper, J. (1985) *Riders*, London, Corgi.

Hancock, T. (1961) *The Blood Donor* and *The Radio Ham* (by Alan Simpson and Ray Galton), Marble Arch Records.

Horne, K. (1975) *The Best of Round the Horne*, BBC Cassettes.

Letts, J. (1983) *A Little Treasury of Limericks Fair and Foul*, Milan, Omega.

Milligan, S. (1973 and 1981) *The Goon Show Scripts* and *More Goon Show Scripts*, London, Woburn Press, and London, Sphere.

Rees, N. (1979/1980/1981/1982) *Graffiti 1, 2, 3, 4*, London, Unwin.

Rees, N. (1980) *The Nigel Rees Book of Slogans and Catchphrases*, London, Unwin.

Index